WELCOME!

Welcome to Hoyle® Card Games, a collection of classic card games for all ages. Hoyle Card Games includes popular trick-taking games like Spades, Bridge, Pinochle and Hearts, challenging melding games Gin Rummy and Canasta, popular favorites Poker and Solitaire (fifty different single deck, double deck and arcade games), family favorites like Old Maid and Go Fish, and more.

You can play most of the games with friends and family members at your computer (head to head) and the witty and personable Hoyle computer characters: Bart, Elayne, Ethel, Gax, Harley, Jasper, Marvin, Maurice, Robin, and Roswell. Each computer character has a unique personality, and you can set characters' skills levels to control how well they play.

Using Hoyle Face Maker, you can create unique pictures (with facial features, hairstyle, clothes, and more) to represent yourself when you play games.

You can customize your game environment by setting the game speed, turning on music and sound effects, and specifying how often the computer characters talk. Set the backgrounds and card backs you like, and choose from four different styles of cards to play with. Within a game, you can set options to make the game easier or more challenging. Statistics are kept for all games, so you can try to beat your best times or beat others' high scores.

No time to finish a game? All of your games-in-progress can be saved and resumed later.

And if you have a connection to the Internet (Windows users only), you can play card games and other Hoyle games with other people around the clock! Internet game play is free (you must have an Internet connection) and easy to set up.

We hope you have as much fun playing these games as we did making them.

Cheers!

—The Hoyle Team

©2000 Sierra On-Line, Inc.
All Rights Reserved.
Printed in the United States of America.

THE HOYLE CARD GAMES TEAM

Producer	Robert Jerauld
Associate Producer	Eric Hook
Designer	Paul Horn
Designer	Robert L. Jerauld
Designer	Rabih AbouJaoudé
Designer	Michael Katz

Principal Software Engineer -
Project Lead	John Gilmore
Principal Software Engineer	Michael Katz
Principal Software Engineer	Mark Seminatore
Senior Software Engineer	Roger Key
Software Engineer	Paul Horn
Software Engineer	Eric Fleming
Software Engineer	Eric Tangborn
Software Engineer	Casey Anderson
Software Engineer	Dennis Ham
Software Engineer	Jonathan Watts
Software Engineer	John Tighe
Lead Artist	Rabih AbouJaoudé
Lead Artist	Julian Love
Senior Artist	Heather Ivy
Senior Artist	Eric Hook
2D/3D Artist	Will Barker
2D Artist	Gayle Rowbotham
Writer, Book Designer	Dana Armstrong
Writer	Michael Jones
Writer	Steven Bryan Bieler
Technical Writer	Nancy Matthew
Script Writer	Jeff Hoyt
Script Writer	Rodney Sherwood
Script Writer	Robert L. Jerauld
Script Writer	Michael Katz
Script Writer	Allen Batchelder
Composer	Mike Caviezel
Composer	Evan Schiller
Sound Engineer	Dennis Ham
Sound Engineer	Mike Caviezel
Voice Synchronization	Dennis Ham
Voice Synchronization	Mike Caviezel
Voice Actor	Allen Batchelder
Voice Actor	Jock Blaney
Voice Actor	Pat Cashman
Voice Actor	Cynthia Doyer
Voice Actor	Amy Frazier
Voice Actor	William Hall, Jr.
Voice Actor	Jeff Hoyt
Voice Actor	M.J. King
Voice Actor	Rodney Sherwood

All voices recorded at
Clatter and Din Studios Seattle, WA

Corporate Product Certification	Dan Neel
Quality Assurance Director	Gary Stevens
QA Supervisor	Laurel Randall
Lead QA Tester	Alex Jacobs
QA Tester	Carlton Thomas
QA Tester	Linda Otis
QA Tester	Phyllis Sherin
QA Tester	Andy Cilley
QA Tester	Bridgett Smith
Bridge and Spades Consultant	Harold E. Van Horn
Vice President of Marketing	Barbara Schwabe
Director of Marketing	Paula Bynan
Brand Manager	Anne Wagner
Associate Brand Manager	Jennifer Arreola
Marketing Communications Associate Account. Mgr.	Melissa Farmin
Senior Public Relations Manager	Michelle Stephens-Jacob
Public Relations Coordinator	Regan Lindstrom
New Business Acquisition Manager	Steve Epstein
Business Unit Manager	Stephen H. Van Horn

CONTENTS

Getting Started	4
One Thousand Years of Playing Cards	5
Bridge	20
Canasta	35
Cribbage	48
Euchre	59
Gin Rummy	68
Go Fish	77
Hearts	79
Memory Match	85
Old Maid	88
Pinochle	90
Pitch	103
Poker	107
Solitaire	115
Spades	126
War	131
Further Reading On Card Games	133
Sierra On-Line Technical Support	134

GETTING STARTED

To start using Hoyle® Card Games, you sign in as a particular player. Different players can be used for different people on your computer, or to change your "identity" when you play. Statistics are tracked for individual players, and games are saved by player name, so you might want to sign in as the same player every time you play.

You can pick a face to represent you while you play games. You can use one of the faces included in Hoyle Card Games, or you can create your own face with Face Maker. With Face Maker, you can choose all the features of your face, and you can even make random faces! You can choose a different face each time you sign in.

You can customize overall options for Hoyle Card Games using the options in the Options menu. Click Environment to customize the game speed, background music, and computer character settings. Click Cards to change the cards and card backs. Click Backgrounds to change the background design that appears while you play.

To start a game, click the picture of the game on the Main Screen or click the Go To menu and select the game name. You also can change between games using the Go To menu.

When you start a game, you will see a Getting Started screen describing the game basics. From this screen, you can change the player lineup, change game options, or read game rules. Click Play to go into the game.

In a game, you can click the game settings item on the Options menu to view and change settings such as the game difficulty, game variations, and the game environment. You only have to set up a game once; your game options are saved for your player. You can also add, remove, and change players by clicking the player in the game or clicking Players on the Options menu.

ONE THOUSAND YEARS OF PLAYING CARDS

"I am sorry I have not learned to play at cards. It is very useful in life: it generates kindness and consolidates society."

— Dr. Samuel Johnson

The history of playing cards begins with sticks.

Imagine, for a moment, that you've gone thousands of years back in time. Not one brick of the pyramids has been laid. Metalworking doesn't exist. Electricity is something that happens only in lightning. The world is a scary place, and you don't understand much about it beyond hunting and gathering.

It's in this world that shamans (those members of your tribe whose job it is to interpret all the scary stuff) try to influence events and foretell the future. To do this, they throw sticks against a cave wall painted with special symbols, or drop them into a ring drawn on the ground, and then try to make sense of the patterns the sticks make. In time, symbols will be added to the sticks, representing animals, plants, gods, people, and the four compass headings. The sticks will evolve into ceremonial arrows.

Cultures around the globe employ the stick method to give themselves an advantage in the fight for survival. And all around the globe, people like you are borrowing those sticks to play games with. There's a simple, practical purpose for almost every other object in your life (knives, spears, clubs, etc.). You use these objects every day, and they hold no mysteries for you. The shaman sticks are different; the symbols, feathers, and other decorations appeal to your imagination.

Eventually special sticks were made just for gaming. As the stick games became more complicated, players recognized the need for a medium more convenient to work with than sticks. But what? And who took this first step?

The Chinese have a better idea

The what was paper, and the who was most likely the Chinese. Both printing and the use of paper money were invented in China in the years 600 to 900. People began playing with the money (as well as spending it) almost immediately, probably because they were already familiar with the idea of a game played with symbols on sticks or some other instrument. (For several centuries Chinese paper money and Chinese playing cards looked almost exactly alike. What effect this had on the Chinese economy is beyond the scope of this book...)

This brings us to the most important evidence we have for the Chinese invention of playing cards—the first recorded mention of cards in world literature, dated 969 and written in one of the Chinese dialects. If we accept 969 as the birthdate of playing cards, then cards are well into their 11th century.

Chinese cards were long and narrow, as were cards in Korea and Japan. In Korea, cards bore on their backs the picture of their ancestor, a feathered arrow (and, remarkably, still do today). Korean suit symbols eventually included man, fish, crow, pheasant, antelope, star, rabbit, and horse. The Japanese developed a dozen suit symbols, although each suit only had three cards. All three of these cultures produced a card common around the world: the wild card, or what English-speaking nations call the "Joker."

India's claim on cards

India can also claim it invented playing cards, though the evidence here isn't as strong as it is for China. No one has found a mention of playing cards in Indian literature that predates 969. There's no smoking gun.

However, it's possible someone in India invented cards without bothering to write about it. The evidence to back the Indian invention theory comes from Chess, of all things. India invented Chess, or rather the ancestor of Chess—that we know. Chess then migrated westward to Persia and eastward to China.

Cards may have followed the same progression. Indian cards were long and narrow, like those elsewhere in Asia, but some kinds of Indian cards were circular and may have been used on chessboards. If the circular Indian cards came first, then perhaps the Chinese converted them into true playing cards after seeing them in action on Indian chessboards.

The consensus today leans toward China as the birthplace of playing cards, but the case for India isn't weak. More on this later.

Playing cards invade Europe

A monk living in the part of medieval Europe that would one day become Germany marked the arrival of playing cards in his corner of the world: "Hence it is that a certain game, called the game of cards, has come to us in this year 1377, but at what time it was invented, or by whom, I am ignorant." The cardplaying monk also noted that "in the game which men call the game at cards, they paint the cards in different manners, and play with them in one way or another." This observation may mean playing cards had been in Europe long enough for different games, and different kinds of packs of cards to have evolved. (As for the phrase "paint the cards," remember, the date of this writing is 1377. Paper is scarce, and the Germans have not yet invented printing with moveable type. Cards were handmade, or, if printed from wood blocks, hand-painted.)

But how did playing cards get to Europe? When last we saw them, they were heading westward from China (or India).

There are four theories to explain how cards arrived in Europe:

1. Brought back from China by the globe-trotting Marco Polo.
2. Brought back from the Holy Land by the slash-and-burn Crusaders.
3. Brought to Central Europe by migrating Gypsies.
4. Brought to Southern Europe by invading Moors and Saracens.

The Marco Polo Theory: Marco Polo and his family traveled in China for 17 years in the late 1200s. When the Polos returned to Italy, they were instant celebrities, and Marco's best-selling account of their Asian sojourn has kept his name alive these past 600 years. It's an intriguing theory, but one without supporting evidence. Marco never mentioned playing cards in his book. (Then again, he never mentioned the Great Wall of China, either. Perhaps he wasn't very observant.) Since no record has come to light to connect any of the Polos with playing cards, this theory is most likely a myth.

The Crusader Theory: The Crusaders fought the resident Arabs for control of the Holy Land off and on from the 11th through the 13th centuries. They could have learned about playing cards from the Arabs during one of the many truces between Crusades. The time period is certainly correct, as the earliest written references to playing cards among the European kingdoms all date from the 1300s.

Unfortunately for this theory, there's no evidence. If the Crusaders played cards, they didn't write home about it. (And we know, from their writings, that they did play Chess.)

The Gypsy Theory: Gypsies are usually associated with the Tarot, cards thought to foretell the future. The first playing cards to cross into Europe were indeed Tarot cards. However, the Gypsies arrived on the scene too late, more than a century after Europeans started writing about cards.

The Moor and Saracen Theory: "Moor" and "Saracen" are medieval-European names for Arabs. The Moors invaded the Iberian Peninsula (site of modern-day Spain and Portugal) in the 8th century, and the Saracens invaded Sicily in the 9th century. These groups maintained a presence on the southern border of Europe for several hundred years, during which time there was considerable trading of cultures. (For example, the Pueblo Indians of the American Southwest learned how to make adobe bricks from the Spanish colonizers, who had learned this trick from the Moors.) We know that Chess came to Europe in this way, and it's most likely that playing cards did, too.

One last bit of evidence: The old Spanish and Italian words for "cards" were "naipes" and "naibi," respectively. Not only are these words nearly identical, they're also quite close to the old Arabic word for cards, "nabi." "Nabi" means "prophet"—a reference to the use of cards to foretell the future.

"The stars foretell, they love you well"

The earliest cards known in Europe were called Tarot. We think of these cards today as being used strictly for fortune-telling, but in the 13th and 14th centuries the Spanish and the Italians were playing games with them, not peering into the future. By the 15th century, Tarot cards had taken on mystical associations, perhaps because of the Gypsy influence. The Europeans began to connect Tarot cards with their home-grown traditions of mysticism, alchemy, and magic. By 1540, when the first book appeared on fortune-telling with cards, the Tarot pack was not being used for anything else.

There are 78 cards in a contemporary Tarot pack—the 52 cards we're familiar with from our standard pack, four extra "court" or "face" cards (these 56 cards are called the "Minor Arcana") and 22 special cards representing various personages, objects, events, and elemental forces (the "Major Arcana"). Early Tarot packs varied in number of cards and in suit markings, but were eventually standardized using an Italian model.

These are the Tarot suits (alternates used at various times are given in parentheses) and what each symbol is thought to represent:

Cups (a Chalice): . . . . .Clergy

Swords: . . . . .Warrior class

Coins (Stars, Disks): . . . . .Merchants

Batons (Sticks, Wands, Rods): . . . .Peasants or workers

This is a point that strengthens the case for India as the cradle of cards, as the four icons of Cups, Swords, Coins, and Batons are also held in the four hands of the Indian deity Ardhanari. Indian playing cards used three of these icons, replacing Cups with a Crown to represent the king. There are no such similarities between Tarot cards and cards from China.

The Church versus the card

European clergy, as a whole, did not graciously accept playing cards (though many men of the cloth were soon caught up in the enthusiasm for card games). The symbols on the cards, as well as the Major Arcana of the Tarot, particularly troubled the Church. Vernon Bartlett told the story in *The Past of Pastimes*:

"It seems reasonable to suppose that, if cards were brought to Europe by the Arabs...they may originally have been used to encourage Mohammedanism or some other Eastern faith; a French pack from the early 15th century has a Saracen as its king of diamonds. So it may be that for this reason, as well as the more obvious one of discouraging betting, the Christian church at one time strongly opposed cardplaying, for subsequently it went out of its way to counter any such heresy by encouraging the use of cards with Christian emblems on them..."

As we're about to see, we owe it to the French for preventing what might have become a holy war over playing cards.

Let them play cards

"However playing cards may have found their way into Europe, and whatever country may first have used them, it is in France that their actual history begins." So wrote Catherine Perry Hargrave in the 1930s in her groundbreaking *A History of Playing Cards*, and all card scholars are indebted to her sleuthing.

Though it's not known when playing cards first appeared in France, we know the French brought to this new amusement the same enthusiasm they devoted to empire-building and fighting with the English. References to cards began turning up in French literature as early as 1328, when the pastime was given equal billing with "Tables" (Backgammon).

In 1392, during the reign of Charles VI, there appeared an entry in the royal account books for a sum of money paid to a local "painter" for three packs of cards "in gold and diverse colors, ornamented with many devices, for the diversion of our lord, the King." (Seventeen of these cards have survived the passage of the centuries and can be viewed in the National Library in Paris; they are all "atouts," or trumps, from the Major Arcana of the Tarot.) That this transaction was recorded as just another everyday bit of budgeting indicates playing cards were well-known by this date.

Given the relative scarcity of paper, the earliest European cards must've been similar to those painted for "our lord, the King"—costly! At first, only the gentry would have been able to afford them, but pastimes have a way of filtering down. The demand for cards would have led enterprising artisans into setting up some sort of mass production of cheaper cards, using stencils and wood blocks. The odds of this having happened are good, as card playing in the last decade of the 14th century seems to have gotten out of hand—at least in the eyes of the authorities. A decree issued in Paris in 1397 forbids working people from playing "tennis, bowls, dice, cards, or ninepins on working days."

The first great French contribution to playing cards

Remember, this is the 1300s. It'll be another century before Columbus sails in search of the Indies; two centuries before the Spanish Armada sails to conquer England; and three centuries before the Pilgrims sail to America in search of religious freedom. "Mass production" in the 1300s would still entail a considerable amount of handwork. How to speed the process? How about reducing the number of cards per pack? The first great French contribution to playing cards, then, was to eliminate the Major Arcana of the Tarot (the Church's primary objection) and the fourth court or face card (it was called the Knight), thus creating a pack consisting of 52 cards.

The second great French contribution

The French next turned their attention to the suit signs (another clerical sticking point). In Spain and Italy, card players were still using the Cups, Swords, Coins, and Batons of the Tarot (and still do today). The Germans had adopted Hearts, Bells, Leaves, and Acorns. But the French invented the symbols that are now the standard in English-speaking countries and much of the rest of the world. Here they are in English, with their French equivalents and the groups they represent:

    Hearts ("Coeurs") . . . . .Clergymen
    Spades ("Piques") . . . . .Knights
    Clubs ("Trefles") . . . . .Farmers
    Diamonds ("Carreaux") . . . . .Peasants

Spades were taken from the point of a lance, though no one knows why it's called a "spade." It's conceivable this is an English mistranslation of the Spanish "espadas," or swords, which suggests a Spanish influence on English cards.

Clubs are clover leaves, a symbol of farming.

Diamonds do not represent money—they represent arrowheads, as used by archers and bowmen. In France at this time, archers and bowmen came from the peasant class.

The third great French contribution

Neither playing cards nor Chess had a Queen when they first appeared in Europe. (There are women represented in the Major Arcana, including an empress and a female pope, but these are special cases. There are no women in the Minor Arcana, the cards most card players are familiar with.)

In India, the King in Chess was supported by a Counselor. In early playing cards, the Spanish, Italians, and French used the King, the Chevalier (a lower nobleman), and the Valet or Knave (meaning, in those days, an even lower nobleman) as the court or face cards. The Germans had a King, an "Ober" or chief officer, and an "Unter" or subordinate. The Spanish or the Italians replaced the Counselor in Chess with the Queen; however, since the French are the ones who condensed the standard pack and dropped the Knight, we can conclude that they're also the ones who replaced the Chevalier with the Queen. Perhaps French card makers were trying to make up for the lost women of the Major Arcana?

The French aren't done yet!

A Frenchman wrote the first history of playing cards (1704).

Deal the English in

We can make an excellent guess as to when playing cards crossed the English Channel. It's very probable that no one in England played games with cards before 1400, and our source for that statement is the poet Geoffrey Chaucer, who died in that year. He spent his writing years chronicling the everyday lives of the men and women around him—and though he often mentioned games (Chess, Checkers, Backgammon), he never mentioned cards.

The earliest reference to playing cards in English comes in 1463, when the cardmakers of London petitioned the King to stop the import of foreign-made packs. This is particularly interesting for two reasons:

1. In 1463, the English weren't making their own paper. They weren't even making their own books—William Caxton, the first man to print books in English, had yet to have his first lesson on the latest hardware (the printing press). And yet, not only were there English cardmakers, there were enough of them to form a political lobby!

2. H.T. Morley, writing in *Old and Curious Playing Cards*, noted that "this express mention of playing cards shows that there must have been a fairly large trade in their manufacture, and that their use was well-known long before." If the English weren't playing cards before 1400, but were buying every pack in sight by 1463, then this pastime had truly swept the kingdom (at a time when the pace of life and the means by which goods, people, and pastimes were distributed were considerably slower than they are today).

The English and the French had just finished fighting the Hundred Years War, leading Morley to theorize that playing cards entered the country by way of English soldiers returning from the front lines in France. The English gentry were no happier to see the "rabble" play cards than the French gentry had been decades earlier. Hargrave found that by 1484, card games had become a major activity among the upper classes, especially at Christmas, and they didn't want to share. In 1495, King Henry VII proclaimed cards off-limits to "servants and apprentices," except at Christmas. (Even then, as Morley discovered, if you occupied the low rungs on the social ladder, you could only play cards in your master's house and, even then, only with your master present.)

His Highness was ignored. Card games became so popular that, in 1529, they even turned up in a sermon, delivered by Hugh Latimer, Bishop of Worcester: "And where you are wont to celebrate Christmas in playing at cards, I intend, by God's grace, to deal unto you Christ's cards, wherein you shall perceive Christ's Rule." (Latimer was burned at the stake some years later, though not because of his pro-card-playing stance.)

As for the English card makers who had petitioned for royal protection, they received that protection and prospered as a result. Hargrave, observing the English social scene less than a century after Latimer's sermon, found that a "fever of gaming" mesmerized everyone from the King on down. Somebody had to make cards for all those people. By 1628, there were enough card makers in London alone to form a guild, grandly named "The Master, Wardens, and Commonality of the Mystery of the Makers of Playing Cards of the City of London."

Hitting the books

While it was the French who produced the first book on playing cards, it was the English who turned books about playing cards and games in general into a publishing phenomenon that continues right through our own time.

The first English books on games with and without cards were part of a series called *The Gamester*, first appearing in 1674. On the world stage, the country that would be the United States of America was still a few tiny communities hugging the Atlantic coast. Boston was barely half a century old; New Amsterdam had been seized from the Dutch and renamed New York just a decade before; and Philadelphia was still just an idea that Quaker leader William Penn was kicking around in the back of his mind.

But England, meanwhile, had survived a brutal civil war and seen the Stuarts restored to the throne. A period of relative peace and increasing prosperity was beginning, and with that prosperity came more leisure time. Hence *The Gamester* series, which proved to be insanely popular. Printed books were still not common, and yet there were often two editions of the same book on games in one year.

The books in this series included *The Court Gamester*, *The Compleat Gamester*, *The Gamester's Companion*, and even *The Polite Gamester*. Many of these books were written by academics skilled in mathematics, and one, published in 1718, was dedicated "by permission" to Isaac Newton.

In his preface to *The Court Gamester* (1734), Richard Seymour provided a simple rationale for learning how to play these games: "Gaming is become so much the fashion among the Beau Monde, that he who in Company should appear ignorant of the games in Vogue, would be reckoned low bred & hardly fit for conversation."

Books on games brings us to the greatest name in gaming: Edmond Hoyle.

Ladies and gentlemen, Hoyle has left the building

> "The only truly immortal human being on record is an Englishman named Edmond Hoyle, who was born in 1679 and buried in 1769 but who has never really died."
>
> — Richard L. Frey, in *The Fireside Book of Cards*

In the world of games, Edmond Hoyle's name is the equivalent of Noah Webster's. One means dictionary, the other means games and their rules. But Noah Webster compiled the first American dictionary. Edmond Hoyle revealed useful strategies for three card games and two board games. To what, then, do we credit Hoyle's immortality? To the lack of copyright laws in the 18th century and to a memorable phrase, "according to Hoyle."

What Hoyle did in the first 50 or so years of his life is not known. By the late 1730s, he had become a tutor of the game of Whist, and, for the edification of his students, he wrote *A Short Treatise on the Game of Whist* (1742). Hoyle's little Whist book was an immediate sensation. It ran through more than a dozen editions in his lifetime, was translated into French and German, and gave Whist such a boost that it became the leading game in England. This forerunner of Bridge soon surpassed in popularity the French games of Piquet and Quadrille (both of which began a nose-dive toward extinction). Wherever Whist was played, people tried to execute the strategies Hoyle had spelled out—in other words, they tried to play the game "according to Hoyle."

Plagiarism is the sincerest form of flattery

Encouraged by this success, the enterprising Hoyle wrote four more "short treatises" and collected them in one five-game volume in 1746. This was the first edition of *Hoyle's Games*. Literary pirates immediately came out with their own books on games, and on each one they slapped the name "Hoyle" without bothering to pay him for the privilege. They also reprinted Hoyle's own book without paying him for that, either. Hoyle tried to fight this tidal wave of piracy, but by the end of the 1700s, there were dozens of these books in print, all by writers not named Hoyle but all published under that name.

Hoyle crossed the Atlantic in 1796, not quite 30 years after his death, when the first book on gaming appeared in America: *Hoyle's Games*, published in Philadelphia. It was, of course, a theft of Hoyle's own book from 1746, with the addition of games Hoyle probably had never played.

Surprisingly, Hoyle (and the other *Gamester* authors) never discussed the rules for playing the games described in their books. "There is a widespread belief that all card games have 'official' rules and that none is genuine that has not first been strained through a man called Hoyle," card scholar David Parlett wrote in *The Penguin Book of Card Games*. "But Hoyle never did lay down official rules. His specialty was guidelines to good strategy."

Richard Frey agreed: "There are countless millions who own one of the innumerable Hoyle books and in whose minds Hoyle is a living man, 'the man who wrote the book,' who probably lives in New York or Los Angeles or Miami or wherever authors live, to whom a letter may be addressed if a ticklish problem arises, and who might even be gotten on the other end of a phone call if the problem were sufficiently urgent."

And so Edmond Hoyle has achieved a curious immortality. His name means "games," and no evidence to the contrary will ever change that. When Ely Culbertson, the man who popularized contract bridge, wrote a book on games, he called it *Culbertson's Hoyle*.

Oh, and the five games Edmond Hoyle actually wrote about? They are Whist, Quadrille, Piquet, Backgammon, and Chess.

In the zone

The English may also be credited with the invention of the playing-card coach. Hoyle (the Whist tutor) wasn't alone, as seen in this passage from a London newspaper of 1753, in which the writer lamented the low state into which parenting had fallen:

> "There is a new kind of tutor lately introduced into some Families of Fashion in this Kingdom, principally to complete the education of the Young Ladies, namely a Gaming Master; who attends his hour as regularly as the Music, Dancing, and French Master; in order to instruct young Misses in Principles of the fashionable Accomplishment of Card playing. However absurd such a conduct in Parents may appear to the Serious and Sober minded, it is undeniably true that such a Practice is now introduced by some, and will it is feared by many more."

American contributions to playing cards

As befits a country of inventors and tinkerers and doers, the American contributions to playing cards are related to their manufacture. Making playing cards was a big business in Massachusetts in the first half of the 19th century, but the actual manufacturing process was still a slow one. Until 1840, the paper stock for the cardboard used to make cards was glued together by hand. In that year, David H. Gilbert, an employee in a playing-card factory outside of Boston, invented a machine that pasted this paper together. Card production skyrocketed.

Card technology leaped forward again in the 1930s, when American manufacturers started printing cards on plastic. This greatly extended the useful life of a pack of cards.

By the way: when Americans speak of a set of 52 playing cards, they usually refer to it as the "deck." The English call it a "pack." When playing cards first came to American shores, people on both sides of the Atlantic were still saying "deck." But as the two countries grew apart, the English began to say "pack" while the Americans kept saying "deck." Using "deck" to refer to playing cards connects you with the era of Shakespeare and to a word the English themselves no longer use.

The evolution of playing-card design, or, Why is a Jack a Jack?

Though playing cards as we in the West know them have traveled a thousand years and thousands of miles, the look of the cards has remained remarkably consistent, especially since the French standardized the suit signs.

In France, the King, Queen, and Jack have usually been based on medieval French figures. There were occasional diversions, as when artists tried to win the favor of the reigning monarch by painting the King of one suit to look like him. The French King of Hearts has also been painted or drawn to represent the biblical Adam, Julius Caesar, Constantine I (the first Roman emperor to convert to Christianity), and Alexander the Great. The King today is thought to be a likeness of Charlemagne.

Though the French Queen of Hearts has never been drawn as Eve or Mrs. Constantine, she has at times represented (or has been said to represent) Helen of Troy (the Jack of Hearts was her lover, Paris), the biblical Rachel, Elizabeth I of England, the goddess Juno, and Joan of Arc. Today the Queen of Hearts is thought to be Judith of Bavaria, the daughter-in-law of Charlemagne. Thus the King and Queen of Hearts in French packs are very possibly pictures of the two hottest celebrities of 9th-century Europe.

There's less variety in face cards in English-speaking countries. Our face cards are all dressed in the style of Henry VII, the founder of the Tudor dynasty. (His years in power, 1485-1509, came a generation or two after the introduction of playing cards in England.) The King, Queen, and Jack represent no one specifically and don't vary from suit to suit.

Attempts to change or somehow improve "the bizarre old figures with which we are familiar" have always failed, Hargrave observes. "Many innovations have been offered from time to time, but they have been popular only as novelties...For serious card playing the unchanging old conventional cards have always been preferred."

A linguistic journey

So, what about that Jack? What exactly is a "Jack"? Remember, the first face cards were King, Chevalier, and Valet or Knave. The Chevalier became the Queen. In England, the lowest face card was called a Knave, which over time changed in meaning from a nobleman of middling birth to a man of humble birth to a rogue (the meaning most of us associate with "knave" today).

Now we go back to the final years of the Hundred Years War between England and France. We're approaching the middle of the 1400s, and England is losing the land it had won in France in the beginning of the war. The English, looking for a scapegoat, turned on a gentleman named William de la Pole, a soldier and statesman. This de la Pole was to blame, they decided, and dubbed him "Jack Napis." Why they dubbed him that is obscure (it might have something to do with a board game played by the "lower" classes), but let's keep going.

The unfortunate de la Pole died in 1450. By 1526, the nickname Jack Napis had been blurred into "jackanapes," meaning a rogue, like the Knave in cards. Soon the Knave was being called the Jackanapes, and then that was shortened to Jack. So every time you play the Jack in a game of cards, you're making a connection with medieval England's doomed attempt to conquer France and one very unlucky individual.

The most unusual use of playing cards on record?

The indefatigable Catherine Perry Hargrave unearthed this story, which she recounts at length in *A History of Playing Cards*. It seems, in the year 1685, the governor of France's Canadian provinces in North America found himself in a difficult position. He was broke, and so was everyone else in Canada. He explained his predicament and what he did about it in a letter to his superior back in France, dated September 24, 1685:

> "I have found myself this year in great straits with regard to the subsistence of the soldiers...I have drawn from my own funds and from those of my friends, all I have been able to get, but at last finding them without means to render me further assistance, and not knowing to what saint to pay my vows, money being extremely scarce, having distributed considerable sums on every side for the pay of the soldiers, it occurred to me to issue, instead of money, notes on playing cards, which I have had cut in quarters...
>
> "I have issued an ordinance by which I have obliged all the inhabitants to receive this money in payments, and to give it circulation, at the same time pledging myself, in my own name, to redeem the said notes. No person has refused them, and so good has been the effect that by this means the troops have lived as usual."

This card-money was issued again in 1686, in 1690, in 1691, and in 1708 (when an issue of card-money even replaced copper coins). In 1719, all card-money was withdrawn and actual French currency reappeared in Canada for the first time in 30 years; unfortunately, everyone was broke again by 1729. Special packs of playing cards were immediately sent from Paris to fill the gap, packs that used a special mark—a coat of arms—to make them hard to counterfeit. The French were getting good at this. Card-money remained in use until 1763, when the French surrendered Canada to the British after losing the French and Indian War. Losing Canada was a disaster for French dreams of empire—and losing the Canadian currency market was equally catastrophic for French makers of playing cards!

BRIDGE

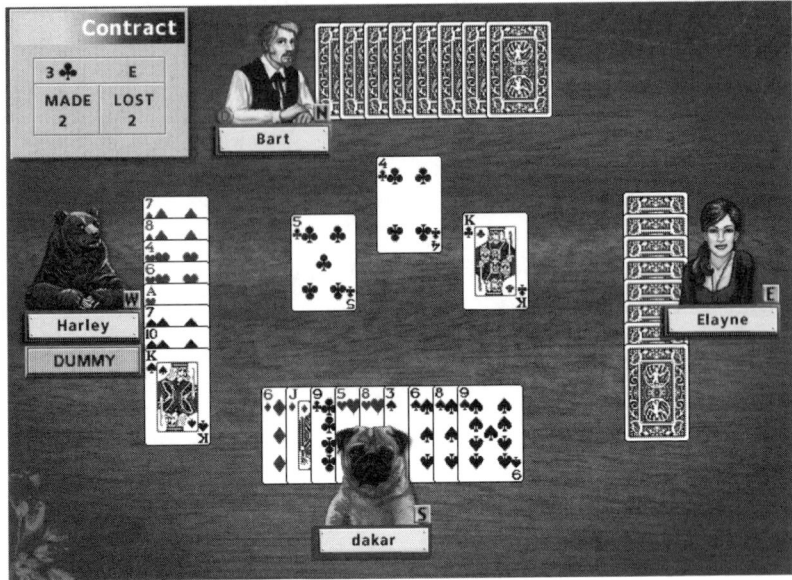

How the game evolved

Bridge is the Chess of card games (and with that statement we will enrage millions of devoted Bridge players, who would argue that Chess is the Bridge of board games). Chess has a long history, and, as befits a game of similar depth and complexity, so does Bridge. Bridge begins with a game called Whist, in a country called England, in an era called "The Restoration."

England's New Deal

In the mid-1600s, the English fought two civil wars, dethroned their king, battled the Scots, the Irish, the Dutch, and the Spanish, dissolved the government when their leader died, and in 1660, restored the monarchy. The new king, Charles II, brought a generation of peace to his people.

Playing cards had been in England for approximately 200 years by then, and the games the English played were caught up in the rush toward recreation. The English had gotten their first playing cards and card games from the French, but now they began to create their own games. They'd been playing a French trick-taking game called Triomphe since the 1500s and had molded it into something of their own. This transformed game was called Trump (a corruption of Triomphe), or Ruff-and-Honours. (Bridge players will note that all three terms, "trump," "ruff," and "honors," are still used today.)

When Charles II began his new job in 1660, Trump was being called Whisk. When he died, in 1685, Whisk was becoming Whist. The following features of Whisk/Whist have been retained by its many descendants:

1. Four players play in partnerships of two.
2. The object is to win tricks.
3. Players must follow suit if possible.
4. A trick is won by the highest card.
5. Any card in a trump suit beats any non-trump.

(In Whist, the last card dealt is turned up; that card's suit becomes the trump suit. It's in the matter of determining trumps that Whist's offspring have found enormous room to evolve.)

What's a "Whisk"?

It's easy to see how a name such as Triomphe could be shortened to Trump, but it's impossible to decipher the means by which Trump became Whist. Catherine Perry Hargrave, in her *History of Playing Cards*, tracked Whist to the expression "Hist, be still!" Whist was supposed to be played in complete silence; you'll recall that in 1495 Henry VII had forbidden the lower orders from playing card games (except at Christmas), so if you wanted to play cards in your master's house the rest of the year, you had better be quiet about it. When Whist was taken up by the card playing gentry in the 17th century, they took silence to be a prerequisite for heavy-duty thinking; ironically, it was really a survival tactic of the poor and powerless.

"Hist, be still!" could easily be compacted into Whist-with-a-t, but we know Whisk-with-a-k came first, "which leaves one just as puzzled," Hargrave wrote.

It's beginning to look a lot like Christmas

It was during the Restoration that the *Gamester* books debuted, and, in them, we can chart Whist's acceptance by a war-weary populace. "Every child almost of 8 years old hath a competent knowledge in that recreation," Charles Cotton wrote of Whist in the first book in the series, *The Compleat Gamester* (1674). Eighty years later, Richard Seymour, author of *The Court Gamester for the Use of Young Princesses*, wrote that Whist "is said to be a very ancient game among us, and the foundation of all English games upon cards."

When Cotton began writing the *Gamesters*, Whist was "as sure a sign of Christmas as frosts and Yule logs," in Hargrave's words. By the time Seymour took over, Whist was a game for every season and everyone, from the unfortunates who swept out the stables to the lord of the manor. Whist also became one of the few, if not the only, English games adopted by the French. The 18th-century philosopher Voltaire was an ardent fan of the game, as was Napoleon.

Rampaging Whist-eria

Whist's ascent to world domination began in the 1720s, when a certain Lord Folkestone and his high-born friends took an interest in it. They began to explore Whist's intellectual depths and were astonished to find them deep indeed. Folkestone and his circle met at a coffeehouse in London, where they conducted the first systematic study ever undertaken of a card game. They then issued the following guidelines to good play:

1. Play from a straight (i.e., your longest and strongest) suit.
2. Study your partner's hand as well as your own. ("Study" as in "deduce what you can.")
3. Never force your partner unnecessarily.
4. Pay attention to the score.

In 1742, Edmond Hoyle published his Whist book, which became an instant best-seller. The worldwide stampede to the Whist table had begun. (Hoyle's adventures in the book trade are given in detail in "One Thousand Years of Playing Cards," page 5).

The exploration of Whist reached its peak in the mid-1800s with a final blast of books, including William Pole's *The Philosophy of Whist: An Essay on the Scientific and Intellectual Aspects of the Modern Game*.

Whist's contribution to lunch

Whist continues to be played today, though compared to Bridge it's barely a blip on the radar screen of recreation. However, Whist players can take pride not only in their game's having given birth to Bridge, but for the impact it's had on international cuisine.

John Montagu was a British statesman of the 18th century. When he wasn't wielding political power, Montagu was busy being a bad boy of the upper classes. He once spent 24 hours straight playing Whist.

During that session, hunger drove him to create a meal from whatever was available. His creation was convenient, portable, and tasty, and soon people all over England were copying him. As the popularity of the new item grew, it was given the name of its creator—John Montagu, 4th Earl of Sandwich.

Biritch: From Russian with love?

The first published report on Khedive, a new card game from the East, appeared in Europe in 1877. The game was believed to have originated in Turkey; it was also popular in Greece and Egypt. Khedive, for unexplained reasons, became Biritch or Russian Whist when it entered France. Khedive is a French translation of a Turkish word for a ruler of Egypt, which was then a province of the Ottoman Empire. And yet, when this game with the French name hit France, it was introduced as a Russian game with a Russian name, Biritch. (Biritch means "town crier" or "herald" in Russian, which is completely unenlightening.)

To further complicate the matter, Biritch (or Khedive) grafted onto Whist an interesting feature from a real Russian game, Vint: instead of turning up the last card of the deal to determine the trump suit, the dealer was free to name as trumps any suit he or she preferred. Bridge was born.

Whist-Bridge: "Bridging over"

By the end of the 1880s, Biritch not only had a new name, Bridge, it had new features as well. These new features are what started Bridge on the road to card-game supremacy (and sent Whist packing):

1. If the dealer chooses not to call trumps, he or she can "bridge" that decision over to his or her partner.
2. A hand may be played without a trump suit.
3. Following the naming of the trump suit (or the decision to proceed without trumps), the dealer's partner becomes the "dummy." The partner's hand is set out face-up and is played by the dealer.

Perhaps Biritch became Bridge because the English word made sense in connection with the game (and because of the similarity in sound). However, a rival theory claims that this early form of Bridge was popularized at a posh club in Bridgetown, Barbados, in the early 1890s, and the name comes from the name of the city. This theory is intriguing but lacking in supporting evidence. Games similar to Bridge were being played late in the 1800s in Denmark, Turkey, Russian, Greece, Egypt, Sweden, and the United States (where it was called Siberia, perhaps because American players still thought the game was of Russian origin).

Whist players were scandalized by the introduction of Bridge in their clubs. Henry Jones, a 19th-century card authority who wrote under the pseudonym "Cavendish," declared, "It is disgusting to find that the Temple of Whist had been thus desecrated." But once-loyal Whist fans were soon flocking to the new Temple of Bridge, and even Jones eventually recanted. Before his death in 1899, he wrote there was "no game of cards in the world wherein skill, sound judgment, and insight into the adversary's methods will meet with more certain reward than they will in Bridge."

When Auction Bridge came along, Bridge was rechristened Bridge-Whist.

Auction Bridge: The game before the game

Auction Bridge most probably began in a lonely outpost of the British empire called Allahabad—a town in India where the local Brits apparently had nothing else to do except invent new card games. One of these gentlemen, Francis Roe, had the thought of bidding for the trump suit (or electing no trump) "as at an auction." In the tradition of Edmond Hoyle, he presented his ideas in a treatise called *The Bridge Manual* (1899) under the unimaginative pseudonym of John Doe.

Auction Bridge introduced the idea of playing two games for the price of one: first the auction, a session of competitive bidding to determine trumps, then the actual play of the cards themselves. Auction Bridge also incorporated the concepts of "undertricks" (tricks you need to make your bid) and "overtricks" (bonus tricks that don't count toward making your bid).

Contract Bridge: The new leader of the pack

Unlike most card games, the invention of Contract Bridge can be traced with absolute certainty to a person, a place, and a date. The person in question was Harold S. "Mike" Vanderbilt, heir to the Vanderbilt fortune, yachtsman, and dedicated card player. Vanderbilt had moved with the times from Whist to Biritch to Bridge-Whist, then to Auction Bridge. Auction Bridge, he felt, had too many drawbacks. He particularly disliked how you could rack up points for tricks you'd won but had never bid on. Vanderbilt had played a

French game called Plafond ("ceiling"), in which only the tricks you'd bid on counted toward winning the game, and this mechanism was much more to his liking.

In November 1925, Vanderbilt and three like-minded friends boarded a cruise ship for a 10-day jaunt from California to Havana via the Panama Canal. By the time they disembarked in Cuba, the voyagers had hammered out, under Vanderbilt's guidance, the basic framework of Contract Bridge. Vanderbilt reviewed some of his thinking in an essay in *The Fireside Book of Cards*:

"My scoring table provided at the outset for lower penalties for a side that had not won a game, to enable it to 'fly the flag' at not too great a cost and to add variety, singularly lacking in Auction, to the new game...We were at a loss for a word to describe a side that is subject to higher penalties. A young lady we met on board—none of us can recall her name—who had played some strange game in California that called for higher penalties under certain conditions, gave us the word used in that game, and 'vulnerable'—what a perfect description—it has been ever since."

Contract Bridge ("Contract" was needed in the 1920s when people were still playing Auction; today's Contract Bridge is by far the dominant form, and is simply called "Bridge") placed great weight on accurate bidding, meaning a new emphasis on strategic thinking. Now, instead of scrambling to take every possible trick, you played to make or break a contract. (In sports terms, the partnership that wins the contract is on offense; the partnership trying to sink that contract is on defense.)

In addition, your bidding during the auction round gives your partner valuable data, and you in turn must deduce what you can from your partner's bidding and from that of the opposition. "The complexity of Bridge lies less in the play than in the use of bidding systems to convey information," David Parlett wrote in *A History of Card Games*. "The most distinctive feature of modern Contract Bridge is that half the game is over before the first cards have been played."

Harold Vanderbilt was by no means modest ("Like the flu, the new game spread by itself, despite the attempts of the old Auction addicts—too old to change—to devise a vaccine to stop it"), but it's not easy being modest when the entertainment you've invented is being played today by millions of people!

Bridge versus Whist: Clash of the titans

Let's sum up the bidding by contrasting the new game with the old:

Bridge	**Whist**
Bid to name trumps	trumps determined by chance
Can play without trumps	always a trump suit
Must win the tricks you contract for	must win a majority of tricks
Only contracted tricks count	everything counts
Extra tricks and bonuses tallied separately	everything counts
Suits are ranked*	all suits are created equal
Use of "dummy" hand	everyone plays own cards
Team that's winning is "vulnerable"	rewards/penalties stay the same

*Somewhere in the journey from Whist to Bridge, the four suits fell into a hierarchy: first Spades, then Hearts, then Diamonds, then Clubs. How this came about is unknown, but it's interesting to note the order of the suits and the groups those suits represented in the medieval French scheme:

Spades	Knights
Hearts	Clergymen
Diamonds	Peasants
Clubs	Farmers

Murder, mayhem, and Contract Bridge

The quips just keep on coming in Jack Olsen's *The Mad World of Bridge* (1960). Bridge is "not so much a game as it is a psychosis." "In the 1930s, America's Bridge players spent an estimated $5 million a year on Bridge instruction, or roughly enough money to pay for 500,000 hours of psychotherapy." But when Olsen wrote of Whist, "Take this simple game, add a dummy, the concept of no-trump, bidding, and an occasional felonious assault, and you have Contract Bridge," there was a smidgen of truth behind it.

In a chapter called "Murder at the Bridge Table," Olsen detailed the many documented accounts of felonious assaults at Bridge tables all over America in the '20s and '30s. Most of these accounts are of husbands and wives bashing each other after particularly tragic misplays. ("Nothing spectacular. Just a typical evening of Bridge as it is played in many homes.") But there were also a number of deaths (and critics claim that *television* causes violence!).

The most infamous case occurred in 1929 in Kansas City when Myrtle Bennett accidentally shot her husband, John, following an argument over a Bridge game. The Bennetts were entertaining their neighbors, the Hoffmans, when the game took a turn for the worse. John misplayed the hand, leading Myrtle to remark on his apparent lack of intelligence. John slapped her, then announced he was leaving. He went to their bedroom to pack. The Hoffmans tried to calm the Bennetts down, but Myrtle and John continued to argue and eventually Myrtle pulled a gun. John ran into the bathroom to hide, but as he was closing the door, Myrtle fired twice. The bullets ripped through the door, mortally wounding John.

Ely Culbertson, the first great popularizer of Contract Bridge, called the affair "a lesson in the importance of precise bidding valuation." Myrtle Bennett was eventually acquitted, and the hand that led to the shooting was eventually published in newspapers nationwide, along with commentary from Bridge experts. Culbertson contributed an analysis called "How Bennett Could Have Saved His Life."

After the hubbub had died down, it was discovered that the newspapers had been hoaxed. The published hand was a fraud. Neither the Hoffmans nor Myrtle Bennett could remember a single card that had been played that night.

There's a lesson in this.

How the game is played

Contract Bridge is played by four people in two partnerships with a standard 52-card pack. The cards in each suit rank from Ace (the highest) to the deuce (the lowest). The suits rank in this order: Spades, Hearts, Diamonds, and then Clubs.

Cards are dealt one at a time, face down, clockwise until each player has received 13 cards.

The bidding or "auction" stage comes next, beginning with the dealer. The various things you can do are known as "calls":

Pass: You may pass rather than make a bid.

Bid: This is your declaration that you intend to win a certain number of "odd" tricks (odd meaning more tricks than six; the first six tricks are called "the book"). You must either name a trump suit or choose "no-trump." The lowest possible bid is one, the highest is seven. (There are 13 tricks in all, but remember that the first six don't count in this process.) For example, you might say "One Diamond," "One no-trump," "Four Spades," and so on.

Your bid must "overcall" or top the preceding bid (if any). This is also called making a "sufficient" bid. Overcalling a bid means you must name a higher number of odd-tricks and/or a higher-ranking denomination: no-trump (high), Spades, Hearts, Diamonds, and then Clubs. One Spade will overcall One Heart; Two Clubs will overcall One Spade; Two Diamonds will overcall One no-trump; etc.

Double: You can double the last bid, so long as one of your opponents made that bid, and no one has yet called a double. What a double does is to double the value of tricks taken. However, if the bid doubled was for, say, Three Spades, any player in the rest of the bidding could overcall it with Three no-trumps, Four Clubs, etc., thereby canceling the double. A particular bid can be doubled only once.

Redouble: A player may in turn redouble the last bid, if a) the bid was made by that player or by that player's partner; b) if the bid has been doubled by an opponent; and c) if the bid hasn't already been redoubled. This further increases the scoring values, but, like the double, it can be canceled by a higher bid. A particular bid can be redoubled only once.

The auction begins when any player makes a bid. If all four players pass the first time around, the cards are thrown in and the next dealer in turn deals. When a bid, double, or redouble is followed by three consecutive passes, the auction is closed. The suit named in the final bid is the trump suit for that hand (if the final bid was a no-trump, the hand will be played without trumps). The player who first bid the suit (or the no-trump) is the "declarer." The number of odd-tricks named in the final bid is that player's "contract."

The player to the declarer's left leads the first card. The declarer's partner then places his or her hand face-up. This hand, and declarer's partner, are called the "dummy." The declarer's partner takes no further part in the hand. The declarer selects the cards to play from the dummy hand.

The object of play is to win tricks. A player is required to follow suit if possible. A trick is won by the highest trump, or, if no trumps come out, by the highest card of the suit led. The player that wins a trick leads the next. Play continues until all 13 tricks have been taken.

Keeping score

Bridge score sheets are halved by a horizontal line. The "trick score" goes below the line; all other scores (usually called the "honor score") go above the line. If the declarer fulfills the contract, winning as many or more odd-tricks than the contract called for, he or she scores below the line for every odd-trick named in the contract. Any trick won by the declarer in excess of his or her contract is called an "overtrick" and is scored above the line.

When a side has scored 100 or more points below the line ("trick points"), it has won a "game." A game may require more than one hand to decide the outcome. The next game begins with both sides back to zero.

A side that has won a game is said to be "vulnerable." A vulnerable side receives increased bonuses in some cases and is subject to higher penalties if it does not fulfill a contract.

Games are played best two out of three. When one side wins two games, they have won the "rubber." All points scored by both sides, both above the line and below the line, are then added up. The side that has the greatest number of points wins the difference between its score and its opponents' score.

The Contract Bridge Scoring System

Trick points (scored below the line by declarer)
Each odd-trick bid & made in ♦ or ♣ 20
Each odd-trick bid & made in ♥ or ♠ 30
First odd-trick bid & made in NT 40
Subsequent odd-tricks, NT 30
If bid was doubled, multiply trick score by two.
If bid was redoubled multiply by four.

Overtrick points (scored above the line by declarer)
Each trick over contract in ♦ or ♣, undoubled 20
Each trick over contract in NT, ♥, ♠, undoubled 30

Hoyle® Card Games

Each trick over contract in any suit:
   Doubled .100 (200 if vulnerable)
   Redoubled . . . . .200 (400 if vulnerable)

Undertrick points (scored above the line by defenders)
Not vulnerable
First undertrick 50
First undertrick, doubled 100
First undertrick, redoubled 200
Second and third undertrick 50
Second and third undertrick, doubled 200
Second and third undertrick, redoubled 400
Each subsequent undertrick 50
Each subsequent undertrick, doubled 300
Each subsequent undertrick, redoubled 600

Vulnerable
First undertrick 100
First undertrick, doubled 200
First undertrick, redoubled .400
Each subsequent undertrick .100
Each subsequent undertrick, doubled 300
Each subsequent undertrick, redoubled 600

Bonus points (scored above the line by declarer)
Making doubled contract 50
Making redoubled contract .100
Small Slam (6 odd-tricks bid & made) 500 (750 if vulnerable)
Grand Slam (7 odd-tricks bid & made) 1,000 (1,500 if vulnerable)

Rubber Bonus:
   If the opponents won 1 game 500
   if the opponents won no games 700

Honors points (scored above the line by either team)
Four trump honors in one hand 100
Five trump honors in one hand 150
Four Aces in one hand (NT contract) 150

Strategies

The importance of learning to bid effectively cannot be overemphasized. A proper bid provides substantial information to your partner, as his or her response should to you. Unfortunately, you are also conveying the same information to your opponents, just as their bidding provides some guide to you as to how you should play your hand to make the bid or defend against your opponents' bid.

Effective bidding of necessity is based on an understanding of what "points" are. The two kinds of points are high-card points and distribution points.

High card points	Distribution Points
Ace=Four points	Void in a suit=Three points
King=Three points	Singleton in a suit=Two points
Queen=Two points	Doubleton in a suit=One point
Jack=One point	

In reaching your total points you cannot count both high-card points and distribution points for the same card. Take a look at this example:

Here, you have a singleton King, normally worth three, but you cannot count three high-card points and two distribution points for the singleton. In this case the best value to assess would be the two distribution points. If your partner bids the suit in which you hold the King, then it would be proper to value it as a King (three points). It is also appropriate to "promote" any other high-card points in the suit bid by your partner one additional point; for example, if you also hold the Jack in that suit it should be promoted to two points.

Opening bids

The opening bid is a team's first bid. The general rule in bridge is that if you have 13 points (combined high-card points and distribution points) and you want a happy partner, you should find a bid somewhere, even if it is in a four card minor suit. Opening bids are invariably on your longest suit. If suits are of equal length, bid the highest ranking suit.

Generally if it is the first (opening) round and your hand has only 11-12 points (combined high-card and distribution points) and you do not have a fairly strong biddable suit (for example, five or six cards headed by at least two face cards and a singleton or doubleton in the other suits) then the appropriate bid would be a pass.

Response to opening bid

If you're a beginner, keep it simple. If you have some strength in a suit your partner has bid, always raise. Strength can be defined as at least six points in your hand and three cards in your partner's suit, as in this example:

♠ A J 8 4   ♥ J 7 6 2   ♦ 10 5 2   ♣ 10 9

This hand contains six points (A, J, J) and at least the minimum three cards in Spades, Hearts, and Diamonds. If your partner bid One Club, however, your hand is too weak, and you should pass.

Any suit of five or more cards is always biddable.

Bidding no-trump

A bid of no-trump is best when you have 15 high-card points, and your hand's distribution is balanced, meaning a 4-3-3-3, 4-4-3-2, or 5-3-3-2 combination. You should also have all suits stopped, meaning you have the Ace, the K-Q, the Q-J-10, and/or the J-10-9-8 in each suit. These card combinations will prevent your opponents from taking a run of tricks in one suit. Most of the time, however, you'll have to make do with "probable" stoppers, such as K-x, Q-J-x, Q-10-x, or even Q-x-x. An example of a hand with stoppers is shown here:

♠ K 2   ♥ Q J 6   ♦ J 10 9 8 3   ♣ A K J

Your 5-3-3-2 suit combination gives you a balanced hand. You have guaranteed stoppers in Hearts, Diamonds, and Clubs, and a probable stopper in Spades.

Playing

If you're the defender and you can't decide what to lead, here's an old bit of Bridge lore: when in doubt, lead the fourth-best card from your longest suit. This is called "leading from length." It's considered the standard way to lead in a no-trump contract, and it's a safe way to proceed in a suit contract.

Typically, an unbalanced hand is more suitable to play a trump contract. A balanced hand is good for a no-trump contract. Whenever a player has a balanced or an unbalanced hand, it is very common for more than one of the other hands to have a similar distribution, and it's something to plan for in the play of the hand. For example, let's say you have the following cards in Diamonds:

♦ A 10 9 7 6 5

If you are defending (your team lost the bid) and have a six-card suit as shown, even though it contains the Ace, there is a good probability that the Ace will be trumped on the first round. The preponderance of Diamonds in your hand makes it more likely someone else has a void in Diamonds. Likewise, if your hand is balanced, it is probable that other players also have balanced hands.

The partnership playing a trump contract should be in command of the trump suit. Decades of Bridge experience have demonstrated that the partners playing the contract should have at least eight trumps between them (the best distributions are 5-3, 4-4, and even 6-2).

The best lead is a card from a combination of top cards in any suit:

♣ K Q J 5

This example, described as KQJx, is very powerful in a no-trump hand (or when it's trump), and should win two or three tricks, despite the lack of the Ace.

When you're on defense, don't lead unsupported Aces (an Ace that has no King, Queen, Jack or ten behind it) unless it's the suit your partner has bid. Suppose you have the following three Hearts:

♥ A 9 2

If it's your lead, you should only play the Ace if your partner bid Hearts. Otherwise, your opponents probably hold the other points and they will win a couple of tricks in this suit. On the other hand, a singleton Ace can be an excellent lead if you have several cards in the suit that is trump. By playing the Ace immediately, you create a void in your hand, increasing the power of your trump cards.

Don't just count cards and points before you begin bidding—try to keep track of them as you play. The bidding, the opening lead, and the play will give you clues to the contents of your opponents' hands.

CANASTA

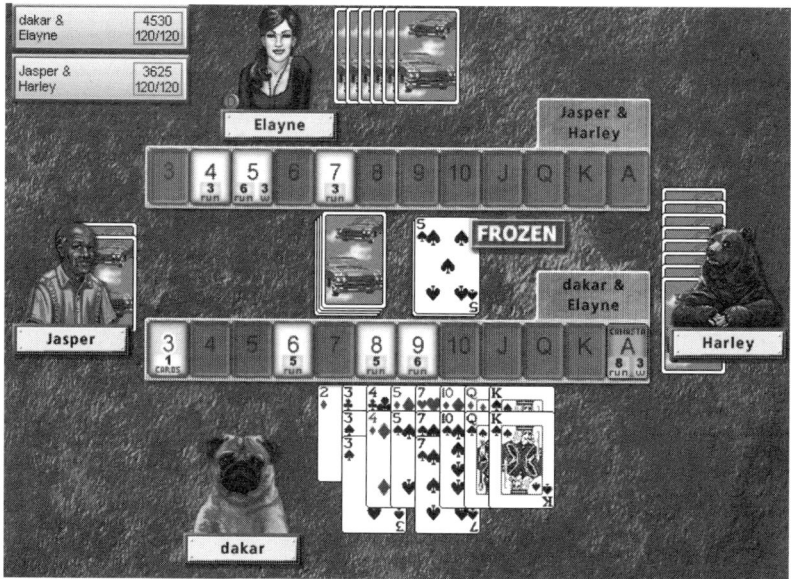

How the game evolved

Canasta is a variant of rummy, the origins of which are discussed in the Gin Rummy chapter later in this manual. The name Canasta means "basket" in Spanish, which probably derived from the basket holding the draw and discard piles; the discard pile is of paramount importance in this game.

Canasta was originally invented in Uruguay in the late 1940s, and soon became popular in Argentina and the rest of Latin America. In the late 1940s/early 1950s, Canasta reached the United States, where it became even more popular than Bridge for a few years; it was probably the most popular card game at any one time. It has since greatly declined in popularity, except for some holdout enthusiasts.

How did Canasta get so popular? It may have been because it has elements of Mah Jongg, another enormously successful game, and as a partnership game, it is easier to learn than Bridge. (Canasta can be played with two, three, or five people, but the most popular version worldwide is the partnership game.)

Derivations of Canasta include Bolivia, Samba, Cuban Canasta and Bolivian Canasta.

Hoyle® Card Games   35

How the game is played

Canasta uses two regular decks of cards, including the jokers (two from each deck). Each player is dealt eleven cards. Players across from each other are partners and play cards to a common area, so each partner can take advantage of the other's play. Canasta is usually played over several hands; the first team to reach 5000 points wins.

Jokers and twos are wild cards and can be used to represent other cards. Black and red threes have special properties.

Rules summary

On your turn, you either draw a card from the draw pile or take the entire discard pile (there are special rules for picking up the discard pile; see "Picking up the discard pile" later in this chapter). You can then play melds and canastas. At the end of your turn, you must discard a card to the discard pile.

Either you or your partner must make an initial meld for your team. Once your team has made its initial meld, both of you can play as many melds and canastas as you want on your turns.

If your team has made at least one canasta, either you or your partner can go out if you can play all the cards in your hand.

Making melds and canastas

Teams score points by making melds and canastas.

A **meld** is three or more cards of the same rank such as 4-4-4, 6-6-6-6-6, or Q-Q-Q-Q-Q. Wild cards (twos and jokers) can substitute for any card, if needed (the only exception is a meld of black threes, which can't include any wild cards). For instance, you could have a meld of 8-8-2. A meld must contain at least two natural cards, and cannot contain more than three wild cards.

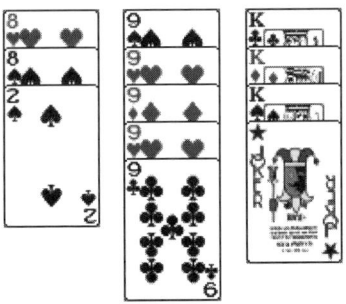

Fig. 1: Examples of melds

Black threes can only be melded as your very last play of a hand before going out.

A **canasta** is a meld which has seven or more cards of the same rank such as 8-8-8-8-8-8-8. Your team must make at least one canasta to win a hand. A canasta can contain up to three wild cards. If the canasta contains only natural cards, it is worth more points.

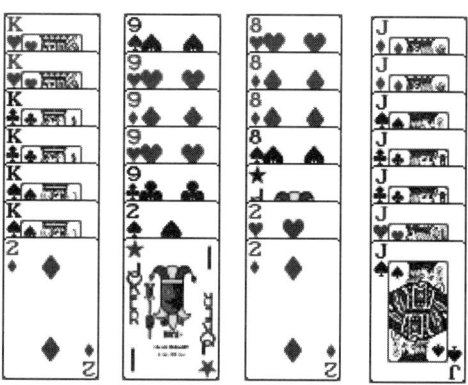

Fig. 2: Examples of canastas

Making the initial meld

The first play your team must make to the table is your initial meld. Either you or your partner must play to the table, in one turn, one or more melds whose point value is equal to or greater than the initial meld value.

Your game score at the end of a hand dictates how many points you need for the initial meld in the next hand. At the beginning of a game, both teams always have an initial meld requirement of 50.

Score	Meld Requirement
0-1495	50
1501-2995	90
3000 or more	120
Negative score	15

This system gives the losing team a better chance of a comeback, since they can potentially play to the table earlier and "go out" earlier. A team with 1600 points must make an initial meld of 90, while the second-place team, with a score of 1250 points, only needs an initial meld of 50.

To figure out whether you can make an initial meld, add up the point values of any cards that you meld:

Card	Point Value
4, 5, 6, 7, and black 3	5 points
8, 9, 10, J, Q, K	10 points
A and 2	20 points
Joker	50 points

The example below (**Fig. 3**) shows a hand that can make an initial meld, given an initial meld requirement of 50. There are two possible initial melds with this hand. You could meld the four Queens (4x10=40) and the three sevens (3x5=15) for a total of 55, or you could meld the four Queens (4x10=40) and the two (worth 20) for a total of 60.

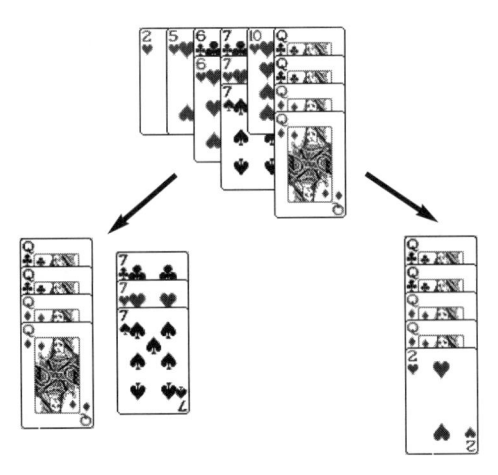

Fig. 3: Initial Melds

Picking up the discard pile

At the beginning of your turn, you can pick up the entire discard pile in certain situations (instead of drawing a card from the draw pile). To pick up the discard pile, you must be able to immediately use the upcard (the top card of the pile) in a meld (either adding it to an existing meld or making a new meld with it using cards already in your hand). You do not get to take the other cards in the pile until you use the upcard in a meld.

Normally, you can pick up the discard pile if you can use the upcard in an existing meld or in a new meld; to use the upcard in a new meld you must combine it with at least two natural cards from your hand or with at least one natural card and one wild card from your hand.

However, if someone has discarded a two, or joker to the pile, the pile is considered "frozen". When the discard pile is frozen, you can only pick it up if you can use the upcard in a meld using at least two natural cards in your hand. In the example below (**Fig. 4**), you can't pick up the discard pile, even though you have a meld of 10s, because you don't have two 10s in your hand.

Fig. 4: Frozen discard pile

A pile stays frozen until someone picks it up.

Important: Before your team has made your initial meld, the pile is not shown as frozen, but you can only pick it up with two natural cards.

You can never pick up a pile if the top card is a joker, two, or black three.

Going out

Your team is qualified to go out (ending the current hand) if you have at least one canasta on the table. To go out, either you or your partner must play all of the cards in your hand to the table. The last card in your hand can either be melded or discarded; this is the only time in the game you are not required to discard at the end of your turn.

When you are ready to go out, you may, if you wish, ask your partner permission to go out. This gives you a way to find out whether your partner wants you to go out, or whether your partner still has a lot of points in his or her hand (that might be used to make canastas) and wants to continue to play. Asking for permission is optional, but your partner's answer is binding; you can only go out on that turn if your partner gives you permission.

Note: It is possible to go out without previously having placed any melds on the table. This is known as going out concealed and is worth extra points. You must be able to immediately play all of the cards in your hand to the table, making your initial meld and at least one canasta. You can discard one card to the discard pile if necessary. Going out concealed is very difficult to do, because you don't get any help from your partner.

Playing the game

At the beginning of the game, one card is flipped to the discard pile. If that card is a two, joker, or red three, another card is flipped on top of it and the pile is frozen. Before play begins, any red threes in players' hands are automatically played to the 3 pile on the board and replaced with new cards.

On your turn, you either draw a card from the draw pile or pick up the discard pile. See "Picking up the discard pile" earlier in this chapter. If you pick up the discard pile, the top card of the pile is automatically played to the appropriate card pile. If the pile was frozen, you must then also play two natural cards to that pile; if you don't, you won't be able to take the pile.

Next, meld cards to the table, if you want to. (The first play your team can make is the initial meld.) You may be able to undo melds, if you need to; see the online help for details.

At the end of your turn, discard a card by dragging it to the discard pile. You must always keep at least one card in your hand at the end of a turn, unless you are going out.

Play proceeds with the player on your left. Continue playing until one team goes out or the deck runs out.

If you're ready to go out, you can go out by laying down all your cards (one card can be discarded, if desired.) If you wish, you can ask your partner for permission before you go out. You can ask for permission after you draw cards but before you play them.

If a player draws the last card in the deck, special conditions apply. If the next player cannot take the discard pile, the hand ends immediately. However, if that player can play the top card of the discard pile to one of his or her team's melds, the player must take the discard pile and play that card. If the player can take the discard pile with a card in his or her hand, he or she can choose to either take the pile or end the hand. In any of these cases, the hand ends, and neither team gets points for going out.

Scoring

Each card you play to the table is worth a certain number of points. These points count towards your initial meld requirement, and are scored at the end of the game. (Note: Any red threes on the table don't count towards the initial meld points.)

Scoring occurs at the end of a hand, after one team has gone out, or if the deck runs out of cards and someone ends the hand. The team that went out gets points for going out, and each team scores points for all the cards they've melded to the table (including the cards in canastas) and any bonus points (points for any red threes and any mixed or natural canastas). Then, any cards remaining in team members' hands (including the partner of the person who went out) are subtracted from each team's score.

Card values

4, 5, 6, 7, and black 3	5 points
8, 9, 10, J, Q, K	10 points
A and 2	20 points
Joker	50 points
Red 3	100 points each (800 if your team has all 4 red threes)

Other scoring

Mixed Canasta	300 points each
Natural Canasta (made with all natural cards)	500 points each
Going out	100 points
Going out concealed*	200 points
Going out before the other team has melded	The other team loses 100 points per red 3 owned by that team, or 800 points if that team owns all four red 3s.

* Going out without having made an initial meld on a previous turn.

Hoyle® Card Games

Strategies

The main reason for making melds is to work with your partner to make canastas. Canastas are worth a lot more points, so focus on making them instead of a number of small melds.

Be careful not to meld too many cards. Having a small hand is a big disadvantage, because you are less likely to be able to pick up the discard pile. However, if your partner has already laid down a meld, it is usually a good idea to play any cards you can to it, so that you can get closer to having a canasta. If you can make a canasta, you should always do it.

Except when making the initial meld and taking the discard pile, avoid adding wild cards to piles (unless you want to finish a canasta). Wild cards are stronger in your hand, since they can be used to make canastas and freeze the pile.

If you have more than three cards you can meld, try just melding three of the cards, holding the others back. This gives your partner a chance to play cards to that meld, but leaves cards in your hand that can potentially pick up the discard pile. It also may let you make a surprise canasta!

Keep track of the discarded cards. If the other team takes the pile, you will want to remember what cards were in it so you can discard safely. Keeping track of discards also gives you an indication which cards the other team are short of.

If you have no choice but to discard a card that lets the other team take the discard pile, stick to low cards (4, 5, 6, 7) whenever possible, since these give the other team less points, and leave more points in your hand for melds.

Strategies for taking the discard pile

A key strategy to Canasta is getting the discard pile and preventing your opponents from getting it, whenever possible. But consider how many cards are in the pile. It is often not worth showing the other team what cards you want by taking a small pile with four or less cards.

Black threes are valuable discards, since they protect the discard pile. Hold on to them until the discard pile is large or something you particularly want to defend.

When the discard pile is not frozen and is full of cards the other team wants, try making safe discards, such as cards that your team already has a large meld of (since you know the other team probably can't meld them). Or discard cards you've already seen the other team discard, or discards they have passed up before.

If the other team has more melds on the table, consider freezing the discard pile, so that you can safely discard cards that your opponents have large melds of.

If the discard pile gets really big, restrain yourself from melding, so that you have more chances to get the pile.

If you're holding cards that the opponents can meld (and you can't), try to discard them when the discard pile is frozen, or when it is small.

Strategies for going out

If you're in a weak position—the other team has melded most of the card ranks, so there are no safe discards, for example—consider going out to minimize your losses.

Asking your partner to go out is sometimes a good way to find out whether your partner can make more canastas. But don't forget that your partner's answer is binding!

If you ask your partner to go out and your partner tells you no, play as many naturals on your turn as possible, holding on to wild cards and at least one safe discard. This gives your partner more opportunities to play cards and make canastas. Holding on to the wild cards means that you are more likely to be able to go out next turn.

If your partner asks you to go out, and you say no (because you have cards left to play), be sure to play as many wild cards as you can on your next turn, and any natural cards that you can use to make canastas (or large melds which your partner could potentially make into canastas). Be sure to keep one card that you can discard safely on your next turn (so that the player to your left can't go out before your partner)!

If all other things are equal, and the other team has three red 3s and the fourth red 3 hasn't been drawn, consider going out as soon as possible. If that team gets the last red 3, they'll get 500 more points! Likewise, if your team has three red 3s, and the fourth red 3 hasn't been drawn, consider postponing going out until you get that last red 3.

CRAZY EIGHTS

How the game evolved

Crazy Eights is also known as Eights and as Swedish Rummy. How it gained a Swedish lineage is uncertain, but Crazy Eights is related to the Rummy family in that players try to rid themselves of their cards by making matches. However, Crazy Eights is classified as a "Stops" game— games in which players are stopped from discarding when they hit a gap in the sequence they're following.

Like most games that look like child's play, Crazy Eights can be traced backward in time to an adult gambling game. The founder of the Stops family appears to be a 17th-century French pastime called Hoc. When Louis XIV took the throne in 1643, the French prime minister, Cardinal Mazarin, faced two problems: a) Louis was five years old, and b) France was running out of money. Mazarin set up a special educational program for the little guy, then tackled the financial crunch by turning the palace into a round-the-clock casino, where 17th-century nobles with more wealth than they knew what to do with squandered it on Hoc.

The start of Stops

Hoc was played in three parts. In the third part, players tried to match all of their cards and be the first to "go out." Eventually, this third part was separated from the first two and became a game in its own right. When Halley's Comet appeared in 1682, the new game became Comet in France and England. All Stops games evolved from this point. In England, Comet was replaced in the 1700s by a new game, by Pope Joan (a Stops game that used a board, like Cribbage), then in the 1800s by Newmarket (named for a race track where the royals congregated).

In America, Newmarket was known as Stops or Boodle. By 1920, this had become Michigan, which was America's favorite game of this type until World War II, when Crazy Eights became the vogue. (The principal difference between Crazy Eights and Michigan is that in Crazy Eights, you draw more cards from the stockpile when you lack the card to make a match.)

How the game is played

Crazy Eights can be played by two, three, or four players.

The game uses the standard 52-card pack. When two play, each receives seven cards; when three or four play, each receives five cards. The remainder of the pack is placed face-down and becomes the "stock." The top card is placed face-up beside the stock and becomes the "starter." All of the discards are placed on the starter, forming the "talon" pile.

Play is clockwise. The first player lays on the starter a card of either the same suit or the same rank. The play continues in turn in the same way. Each card played (other than an eight) must match the top card of the talon pile in suit or rank.

A player unable to follow suit or rank must draw cards from the top of the stock until he or she can follow. A player may draw from the stock even if able to play without it. After the stock is exhausted, a player unable to play passes, and the turn passes to the left.

As the name of the game implies, all eights are wild. An eight may be played at any time, even if the player could legally play another card. If you play an eight, you designate a suit, and the next player must play a card of that suit or another eight.

Play ends when a player gets rid of his or her last card, if the game is "cutthroat" (as in **Hoyle Card Games**). In partnership play, the game ends when both players on one side have gone out.

If the stock is exhausted and no one can play a legal card, the game ends in a "block." This is a no-win hand.

The player or side that goes out collects points for all cards remaining in the hands of the opponents: 50 for each eight, 10 for each face card, one for each Ace, and the regular value for the remaining cards. If two players tie (in three-hand play), they split the winnings.

Strategies

Unlike many of the classic American games, in Crazy Eights you want to "avoid a void," or you'll have to draw more cards from the stock. A balanced hand is best, so you'll generally want to play cards from your longest suit. In **Fig. 1**, your best option is to transfer the suit to Diamonds by playing the 10 of Diamonds.

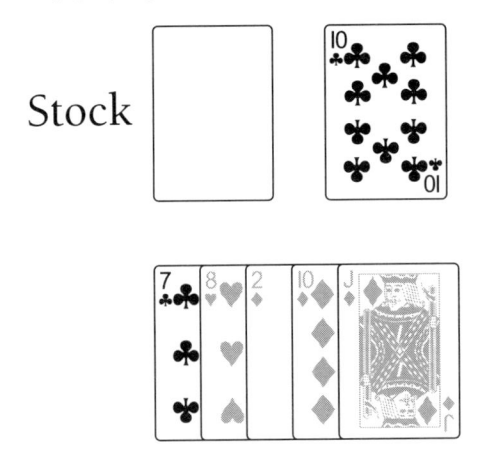

Fig. 1: Playing your longest suit

At the end of the game all cards remaining in the losers' hands are counted up and added to the victor's score. For this reason, play your higher cards whenever possible. Your 8s are the only exception. These cards are most useful at the end of the game, when you'll be running out of suits (and therefore options), so don't play them except to avoid drawing from the stock. If you do hang onto your 8s, you will also need to watch the other players. If someone gets down to their last card, make sure you play the 8 immediately to avoid giving away 50 points to the winner.

The most devious tactic you can employ in Crazy Eights is to observe opponents who are down to their last few cards. **Fig. 2** shows an example of this. The 5 of Diamonds is showing. After being forced to draw a card, the player on the right plays the new card immediately. By drawing, this player has revealed a void in Diamonds. You play your 8 and change the suit to Diamonds. This decision is designed to thwart your opponent, as it doesn't obviously benefit you. However, if you can force the leading player to draw several cards, you'll be more likely to win the game yourself.

If you have a strong need to win, you can try counting cards in order to deduce what your opponents are holding when the stock is exhausted. If you think keeping track of 52 cards is hard, play a few hands of Bridge for practice.

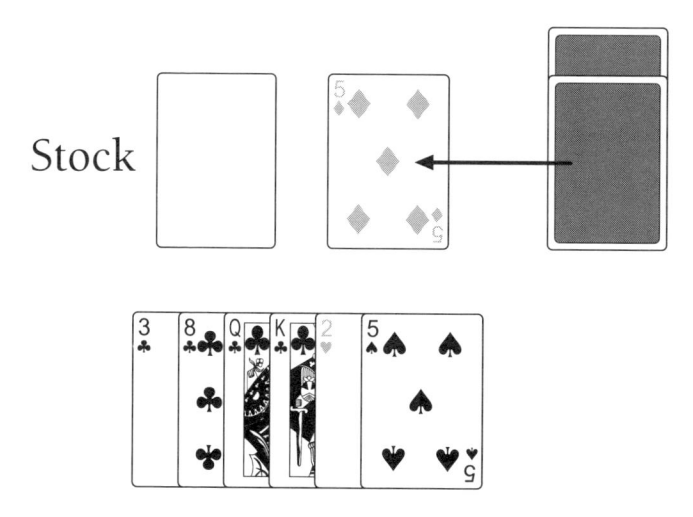

Fig. 2: Stopping a win

CRIBBAGE

How the game evolved

Cribbage pops up in recorded literature early in the 17th century. Frederic Grunfeld in *Games of the World* traced it to an English card game called Noddy. (No one knows how Noddy was played, but in the 1600s, the word meant a "fumbling, inept person," so the reader is welcome to draw a conclusion from that.) Noddy was the only card game of that era that used a board for scoring, and, as there are no other contestants for the title, we can say with some assurance that this long-forgotten card game probably inspired Cribbage.

The game was quickly taken up by "gentlemen gamblers" throughout Europe, which lends some credence to the claim that Cribbage was invented (or at least popularized) by Sir John Suckling (1609-1642), poet, soldier, gentleman gambler, and ne'er-do-well. (Suckling himself never made this claim; it was made instead by a contemporary writer named John Aubrey in a book called *Brief Lives*.)

Few changes have been made in the rules since Suckling's time, beyond the introduction of a four-handed variation. In two-handed Cribbage, you're dealt six cards; in Suckling's day it was five. There's also a seven-card variety. Today, two-handed, six-card Cribbage is the most popular way to play.

Cribbage on the world stage

In the early 1800s, the king of Sweden, Adolf Gustav IV, made several miscalculations in the realm of foreign affairs. Sweden soon found itself at war with almost everyone in Europe, and the Swedish military leaders, justifiably alarmed, forced the king to abdicate. Gustav signed the abdication papers on a Cribbage board, which perhaps he had dedicated too much time to.

The hard life of a filthy-rich poet

John Aubrey described Suckling as "the greatest gallant of his time, and the greatest Gamester, both for Bowling and for Cards...He played at Cards rarely well, and did use to practice by himself a-bed, and there studied how the best way of managing the cards could be." Aubrey, however, didn't set out merely to burnish Suckling's reputation. He also chronicled the gentleman's talent for cheating. Suckling had inherited a fortune at 18, and one of the uses he put this money to was to make his own packs of marked playing cards. He sent these packs as gifts to all the gaming places in England where gentlemen congregated. Of course, when he arrived, he fleeced the lot!

In 1639, England went to war against Scotland, and Suckling, perhaps wanting to do the right thing, raised his own regiment, paying for their horses (and their gaudy uniforms) from his Cribbage winnings. Suckling's commandos fared poorly against the Scots, but they looked great.

Suckling's poetry was witty, lively, and ahead of his time in its use of everyday language. He seemed to especially enjoy puncturing the high-flown pretensions of literary love ballads:

> *Out upon it I have loved*
> *Three whole days together;*
> *And am like to love three more,*
> *If it prove fair weather.*

In 1642, Suckling took part in a failed attempt to free a friend from a jail cell in the Tower of London. He was forced to leave the country, and he died later that year in Paris, possibly by his own hand.

How the game is played

Cribbage is a game for two to four players; since **Hoyle Card Games** uses the two-player version, we'll confine ourselves to that. The game uses the standard 52-card pack. The cards in each suit rank from the King (the highest) down to the Ace (the lowest). In "counting" or numerical value, the King, Queen, Jack, and 10 each count for 10 (and so are called "tenth" cards), the Ace counts as one, and the other cards are face value.

The game operates on the principle of matching combinations of cards: pairs, three or more of a kind, flushes, "runs" (sequences), and groups of cards that add up to 15. Players score points for matching both during and after play (after play, points are totaled for combinations in hand). The first person to score 121 points is the winner.

Cribbage also uses a "cribbage board," a rectangular panel with rows of holes that form a sort of track. At one end, or in the center, you'll find three additional holes, called "game holes." Each player has two pegs, which are placed at the start in the game holes. After each hand, the player advances a peg an appropriate number of holes (one hole per point) away from the start (assuming that that player scored any points). The player's second score is recorded by placing the second peg an appropriate distance ahead of the first. For each subsequent score, the peg in back jumps over the peg in front. The distance between the two pegs always shows the amount of the last score. This method holds math mistakes to a minimum.

Each player receives six cards, dealt one at a time. After looking over the hand, each player "lays away" two cards face-down. The four cards laid away, placed in one pile, form the "crib." The crib, also called the "kitty," counts for the dealer (the dealer always has an advantage in this game). The non-dealer therefore tries to lay away "balking cards"—cards that are least likely to create a score in the crib.

To begin play (called "pegging"), the dealer turns up the top card of the stock. This card is called "one for the starter." If this card is a Jack, the dealer immediately "pegs two" (advances his peg two spaces), traditionally called "two for his heels."

The non-dealer begins the play by laying a card from his or her hand face-up on the table, announcing its value. The dealer does the same (each player discards to his or her own pile). Play continues in the same way, by alternate exposures of the cards, each player announcing the new total count. The total may not be carried past 31.

If a player adds a card that brings the total exactly to 31, he or she pegs two. If a player is unable to play another card without exceeding 31, he or she says "Go," and the second player must play as many cards as possible up to but not more than 31. The player who plays the last card under 31 scores a point. The discard process begins again from zero.

After the hands have been emptied, the totals of any matches in the discards (including the starter card) are counted and added to each player's score. The non-dealer scores first. The dealer then scores and also scores the crib. Any Jack of the same suit as the starter card scores one point (for "nobs").

One game option is called Muggins, which means that if your opponent forgets to claim any points, you're allowed to yell "Muggins!" and claim the points for yourself. (The knowledge of who or what a Muggins is has long been lost to us. The word is also used in a form of Dominoes, though with a different meaning.)

These are the most usual point scores:

In Play

Total of 15	2
Pair	2
Three of a Kind	6
Four of a Kind	12
Run of three or more	1 per card
Turned-up Jack	2
Go	1
Total of 31	2

In Hand

Total of 15	2
Pair	2
Three of a Kind	6
Four of a Kind	12
Run of three or more	1 per card
Flush (four cards)	4
Flush (five cards)	5
Nobs	1
Double Run of Three*	8
Double Run of Four*	10

Hoyle® Card Games

Triple Run* .15
Quadruple Run* 16

*A **Run** is a sequence of cards such as 6-5-4.

A **Double Run of Three** means one duplication in a sequence of four: 6-6-5-4.

A **Double Run of Four** is one duplication in five cards: 7-6-6-5-4.

A **Triple Run** is one triplication in a sequence of five: 8-7-6-6-6.

A **Quadruple Run** is two duplications in a sequence of five: 8-8-7-7-6.

Strategies

If you're just beginning at Cribbage and you're not sure what to discard, here's a prescription for improving your play—focus first on building your hand. Begin by looking for combinations of 15. 5s are especially prized because a third of the deck is made up of cards with a value of ten (10s and face cards), making lots of easy 15s. Any sequential cards are good (runs are easy to get and score relatively well). Combinations of 7 and 8 are very powerful, because in addition to scoring potential on runs, they also add up to 15. Pairs score easy points and are often (not always) worth keeping.

After considering the hand you'd like to keep, turn your attention to the crib. If it's your crib (i.e., you dealt), see if you have two good cards that can't be easily joined to the rest of your hand. If you do, discard them. For example, the 3 and 4 in **Fig. 1** aren't scoring at all right now. By putting them in the crib, you're liable to score on 15s, pairs, runs, and double runs.

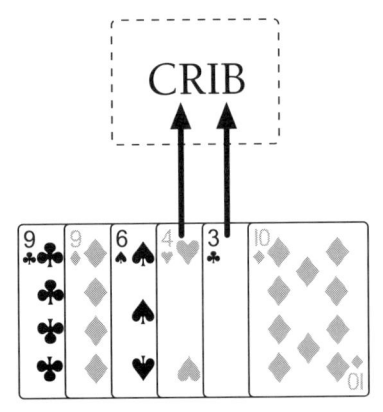

Fig. 1: Discarding to your crib

If it's your opponent's crib, be cautious about giving away cards that could be easily turned into big points. Avoid giving any 5s or any of the card combinations already mentioned (15s, sequences, and pairs).

Fig. 2 shows a situation requiring some careful thinking. Keeping the 5, 6, 7 (run for three) and King (K + 5 = 15) seems most obvious. But consider this: should you give away the Ace and 3 when you may be contributing to a possible run (if the other player obtains a 2) in your opponent's crib? Discarding the King and the Ace is a better alternative, because you can avoid the risk while still keeping two points (7 + 3 + 5 = 15). Be on the lookout for triple card combinations of 15 like this.

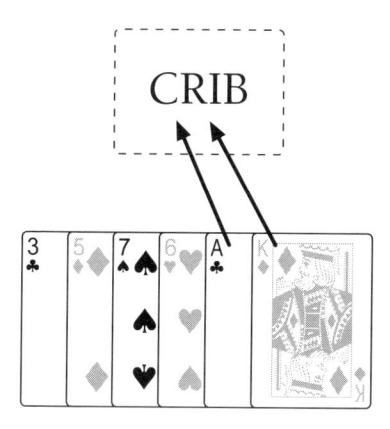

Fig. 2: Discarding to your opponent's crib

Fig. 3 shows a situation requiring even greater caution. Let's suppose it's your opponent's crib. Your two 5s aren't scoring anything, but discarding 5s is not deemed wise in general (especially two of them!). Two 5s could contribute to a huge crib for your opponent (4-12 points is most likely, but it could be over 20). Balking (intentionally ruining) your score may be the best course of action to prevent your opponent from hitting it big. The horrifying reality is that, if you don't discard both of the 5s, you'll have to break up a majestic hand (already worth 8 to 24 points!). In this situation, consider the overall score. Is it the right time to take a risk? Take a look at the board. If you're far behind, maybe you should go ahead and do it. If you're far ahead, why chance it? Make sure you weigh these additional factors before you make a decision.

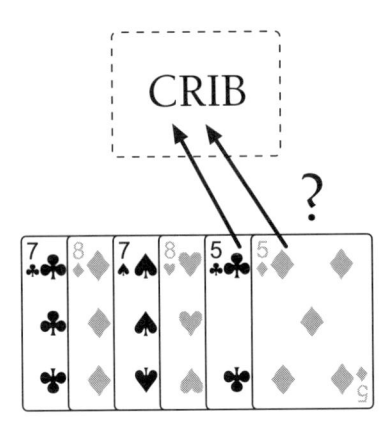

Fig. 3: Discarding in the end-game

When play begins, avoid leading with cards that allow easy points by your opponent, especially 5s. Any time that you lead with a 5, your opponent is likely to play a 10 or face card for an easy two points.

You can also try to create scoring opportunities by trapping your opponent. For example, if you lead with one card in a pair (**Fig. 4**), your opponent may respond with a matching card in order to score two points. Now you spring the trap, playing your second 6 and pegging six points for three of a kind.

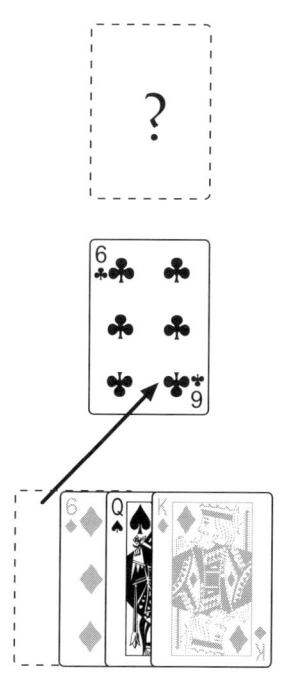

Fig. 4: Trapping your opponent

At the end of a game, if you are ahead and about to peg out (win), you can discard for a good pegging hand. This means you want cards that will allow you combinations of 15 on almost any card your opponent plays. For example, a 5, 6, 8, 9 isn't normally a great hand, but it gives you great odds of scoring two points on a 15.

The exception to this when you play the first card (i.e. when the other player deals), in which case it is more difficult to score. In this case, it's better to hold onto an Ace or another low card to make sure you can play as the count approaches 31.

Conversely, if your opponent is about to peg out, play a low card so as to make 15 unreachable. If you're dealt an Ace, keep it so they won't easily get the "Go" for a point.

Advanced Strategies

Since the highest points are obtained when scoring the hands, it is easy to think that pegging one or two points at a time during play is small potatoes. However, all other things being equal, a good pegger will usually win at Cribbage. It's a case of the tortoise and the hare—slogging it out for the little points really adds up.

Performing well during pegging involves a mental effort. Look at **Fig. 5**. Your opponent leads with a 3. You respond with a 9. The 9 is a good play, taking into account that a second 9 is showing as the starter card (out of play); it is unlikely your opponent can play another 9, scoring two points on a pair.

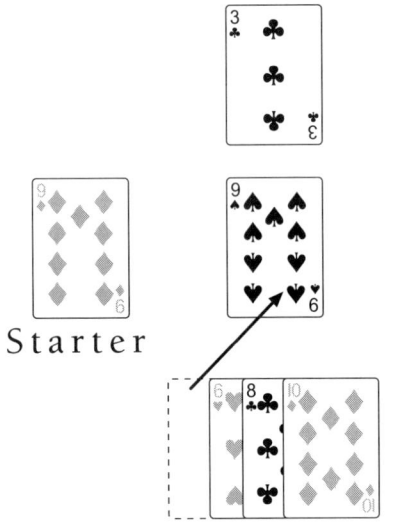

Starter

Fig. 5: Example of play

Fig. 6 shows that a 2 is played next. The total is 14. Any of your remaining cards seems acceptable at first glance. The 6, however, would make a total of 20. In general, leaving a count of 20 is undesirable (unless you have an Ace in hand) because of the high probability of 10s and face cards. Of course, leaving 21 is even worse and is likely to lead to an easy two points for your opponent.

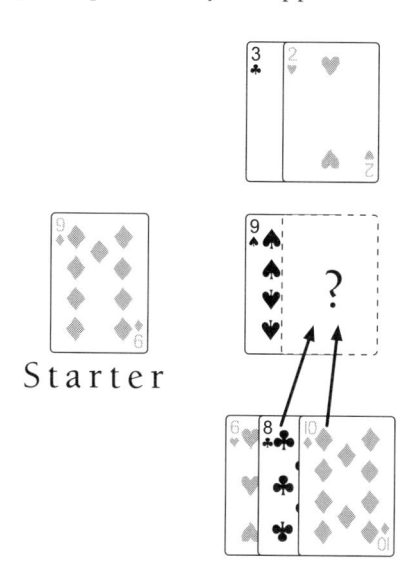

Fig. 6: Example of play (2)

Additional information can be gleaned from this illustration, based on the 3 and 2 that have been played by your opponent. Remember: you're not the only one trying to build strong hands through your initial discards. The 3 and 2, adding up to five, may indicate that he or she has one or more 10s still in hand. In view of this, it is even more critical to avoid playing the 6. Your opponent may also be holding one or more of Ace, 2, 3, and 4, as part of a run.

Continuing with this example, **Fig. 7** shows what happens next. You have played the 8, and your opponent, as suspected, counters with a 4. The total is 26. You say, "Go" and your opponent scores one point. Don't miss this important information; your opponent could not play any cards adding up to 31 or less. This means that your opponent does not have any cards from Ace to 5. The only other cards that would help your opponent's hand significantly is any face card (3 + 2 + 10 = 15), a 10 (for 15), a 9 (2 + 4 + 9 = 15), or a 6 (3 + 2 + 4 + 6 = 15).

Fig. 7: Example of play (3)

You lead the next round, and you have a choice between your last two cards, the 6 and 10. This is a close call, but playing the 10 is the best move (**Fig. 8**). It's not a risk, because you know the other player can't have a 5. Playing the 6 would allow the other player to score two points by playing a 9 (if they have one).

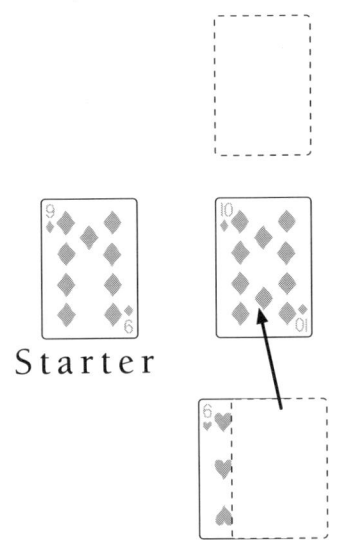

Fig. 8: Next round

EUCHRE

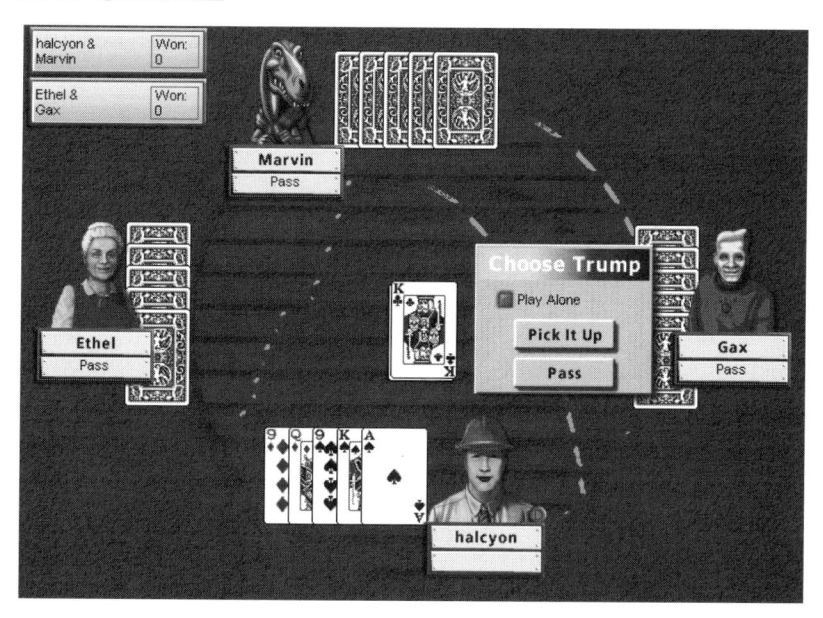

How the game evolved

"Those who are familiar with life in the United States must be aware of the enormous popularity that the game of Euchre enjoys, in one form and another. Before the advent of Bridge it was the national game, if we omit Poker."

—R.F. Foster, 1909

Euchre was once to the United States what Whist was to Great Britain. Merilyn Simonds Mohr estimates in *The Games Treasury* that by the country's centennial, two-thirds of all Americans knew how to play Euchre. Whist was swept aside by the barrage of Bridge, but Euchre survived Poker and Rummy, and still enjoys a loyal following.

A French-German collaboration

Euchre, which was written about as early as 1829 (in connection with riverboat gambling on the Mississippi), is a trick-taking game with restrictions. In the case of Euchre, these restrictions are the use of a "short" pack, just 32 cards, and a hand of just five cards. It can be traced with fair certainty to two games. The first is the French game of Triomphe, which seems to have given birth to most of the trick-taking games we play today. The second is a game called Jucker or Juckerspiel, which developed in a region that has sometimes been French, sometimes German—Alsace, in northeastern France.

Because of its French-German ancestry, Euchre slipped into the United States in two ways, through the French in Louisiana and through the Germans in Pennsylvania. The German influence is most evident in the word "Bower." In modern Euchre, the highest card is the Joker, also called the "Best Bower;" the second-highest is the Jack of Trumps, or the "Right Bower;" and the third-highest is the Jack of the suit that's the same color as trumps, also known as the "Left Bower." Bower, in this case, is not the English-language "bower," which we use to mean a shady spot in a park or a garden. The Bower in Euchre is the English spelling of the German "bauer" or the Dutch "boer," which in those languages means "farmer" or "jack."

Euchre made the big time in 1863, when it was at last admitted to the pages of *Hoyle*.

The "Imperial Trump"

The German influence on Euchre might also be present in the word "Joker," as this might be an Americanization of the German Jucker. The Joker is first mentioned in connection with Euchre in the book *Euchre: How to Play It* (1886). The first mention of the Joker in Poker is a decade earlier— *The American Hoyle* (1875)— but it may be that Euchre was the game for which the Joker was invented, not Poker. (Part of the confusion on this issue might have come from the simultaneous spread of both games northward on the Mississippi.)

Euchre: How to Play It included a description of a game called Railway Euchre in which a 33rd card, "the Joker, or Imperial Trump," is used. But Catherine Perry Hargrave, in *A History of Playing Cards,* found even earlier Jokers, from 1862 and 1865. The 1862 card has a tiger on it and the label "Highest Trump," while the one from 1865 is inscribed "This card takes either Bower" and "Imperial Bower, or Highest Trump Card." David Parlett confirmed Hargrave's discovery, noting in *A History of Card Games* that American playing-card manufacturers didn't start including a spare card in all their packs until the 1880s. "It was presumably only when [Jokers] were customary in full-length packs that Poker players started using them as wild cards." Incidentally, the Joker we know as the court jester didn't assume that costume until the turn of the century.

It's a wonderful life

R.F. Foster, quoted above, spent a happy life in the service of playing cards. He invented Whist's "Rule of Eleven," a popular signaling device between partners; wrote at least one *Hoyle* (*Foster's Complete Hoyle*, 1897); and edited the United States Playing Card Co.'s annual *Official Rules of Card Games* from the turn of the century until just after World War I. Parlett claimed Foster invented "Five Hundred," a Euchre variant with bidding, in the 1890s, the idea being to attempt to do to Euchre what Bridge did to Whist. Five Hundred never caught on in this country, but it's quite popular in Australia.

How the game is played

Four people play in two partnerships. Euchre uses the standard 52-card pack, but with 28 cards removed (everything below the 9). **Hoyle Card Games** does not use the Joker.

The rank of cards in each non-trump suit: Ace (the highest), King, Queen, Jack, 10, 9 (the lowest).

The rank of cards in trumps: the Jack of the trump suit (the Right Bower) followed by the Jack of the same color (the Left Bower). For example, if Hearts are trumps, they would rank as follows: the Jack of Hearts, Jack of Diamonds, and then the rest of the Hearts. The trump suit always has seven cards; the next suit (same color as the trump suit) has five; and the "cross" suits (opposite color as the trump) each have six.

Five cards are dealt to each player. The pack is placed face-down, with the top card turned face-up. This card determines the trump suit for the deal.

The first player may either pass or accept the turned-up card as trumps. If the first player passes, the next player faces the same decision, and so on. As soon as a player accepts the turned-up card as trumps, the dealer discards a card. The discard is placed cross-wise under the undealt cards. The turned-up card belongs to the dealer in place of the discard.

If all players pass, the first player then has the right to name the trump suit, or to pass. (If the first player passes, the next player has an opportunity to name a trump suit, and so on.) The suit of the rejected card cannot be used for trumps. If all players pass a second time around, the cards are thrown in for a new deal.

The player who declares the trump suit has the right to play alone. The partner of this lone wolf lays his or her cards face-down and does not participate in the hand.

In play, players must follow suit of whatever card is lead (if able). A trick is won by the highest trump or by the highest card of the suit led. The winner of a trick leads the next card.

The object is to win at least three tricks (of a possible five). If the side that called trumps fails this, it is "euchred." The winning of all five tricks is called "march."

In the traditional scoring, the side that called trumps wins one point for making three or four tricks; for making five tricks or march, they score two points. For the person playing alone: three or four tricks gain one point; march nets four points. If the side that called trumps is euchred, their opponents win two points. Four-hand euchre is usually played for a game of five points.

Strategies

Don't be in a hurry to become the declarer and order up trump. While ordering up trump is a huge advantage, remember that if you can't take three tricks, your opponents gets two points (that's what you call a big troll lurking under the bridge). Euchre is supposed to be a fun game, right? Do you really want to sweat that hard for your third trick? If you only think you can take two tricks, consider passing. Give your opponents an opportunity to do the sweating instead.

So when is your hand good enough to order up trump? Easy answers are a little scarce, but here's a couple of ideas: your partner will take one trick on average. That means you want an assurance of at least two tricks yourself—and three is better. "Takers" (winning cards) are Aces and the higher trumps (Bowers, Ace, King). **Fig. 1** shows an example of a good hand. Declaring trump will give this player two higher trumps (the Right Bower and the King) and one Ace. This should be good enough for at least two tricks, maybe three. With three takers, don't hesitate to order up trump. It's a safe bet.

upturned trump

Fig. 1: Example of a good hand

Three trumps of any rank form a very powerful hand. You can quickly force out all the highest trumps and subsequently win a couple of tricks.

Be sure you have an unbeatable hand before opting to play alone. Otherwise, let your partner help you out. Your odds of gaining extra points (for winning five tricks) is much greater with a partner. For example, the player in **Fig. 2** has a great hand but is missing the Left Bower (Jack of Diamonds) and the Ace of Hearts. This gap could potentially cost the player one trick. However, if the player's partner has the other Jack, he or she could still take everything.

upturned trump

Fig. 2: Playing alone

Hoyle® Card Games

It's war when play begins. Fight for every trick as if your life depended on it. If you think you can take a trick, do so. **Fig. 3** shows a typical situation. Suppose in this example that you are First Hand (first player). You have two decent cards (an Ace and a low trump), and three garbage cards. If you play the Queen (your trump), she will certainly go down at the hands of a superior trump. Save it for later.

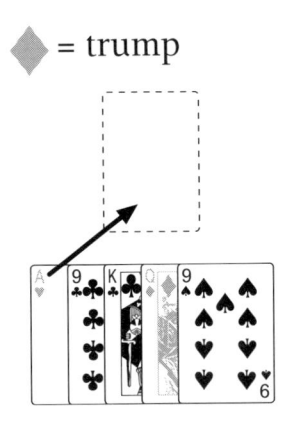

♦ = trump

Fig. 3: First Hand options

If you play a garbage card, you will lose the trick and may never get the lead back. Your Ace of Hearts is the best option. It's like firing your derringer—you've only got one shot. If you play it now, you can force out all the Hearts and (if you're not trumped) win the trick.

In the Old West, the fastest gun was always the most feared. The first to trump will often win a given trick. Because there are only five cards in each player's hand, you won't have much time to void your suits, so absolutely do not pass up any early trumping opportunities.

Advanced Strategies

When weighing trump, always keep in mind which player is the dealer. **Fig. 4** shows a situation in which Jack of Diamonds is upturned as the possible trump. You're holding the hand shown. If your partner is dealer, don't pass this opportunity to order it up. It will give him the Right Bower (Jack of Diamonds), give you the Left Bower (Jack of Hearts), along with a couple of trumps. It's a can't-fail proposition. You and your partner may even take five tricks.

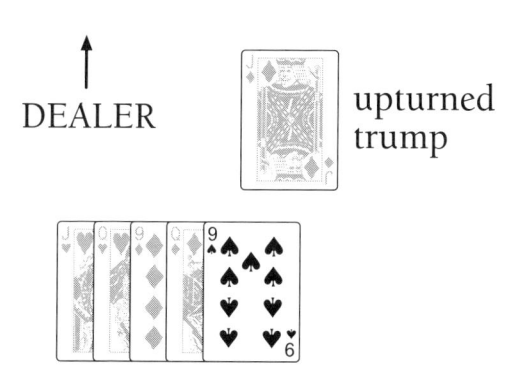

Fig. 4: When to order up

Consider how drastically this situation changes if your opponent on the left is dealer. If you order it up in this case, you may still take some tricks, but you won't take five. By giving up the Right Bower, you're also giving up at least one trick.

Your Kings and Aces are better with a "backer." A backer is a lower card of the same suit. **Fig. 5** shows a hand in which the 10 is backing up the Ace. Hearts are trump. **Fig. 6** shows how this can come in handy. In this situation, the First Hand (player to the dealer's left) leads with the Right Bower, forcing out the Left Bower. The last player sacrifices the 10 and saves the Ace of Hearts for a later hand. Even the unreliable King is more likely to take a trick when backed up.

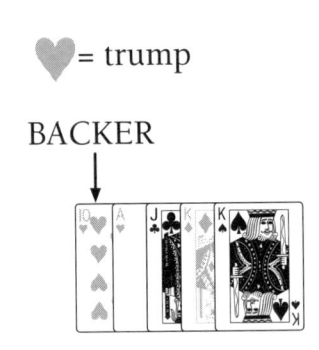

♥ = trump

BACKER

Fig. 5: 10 backing Ace

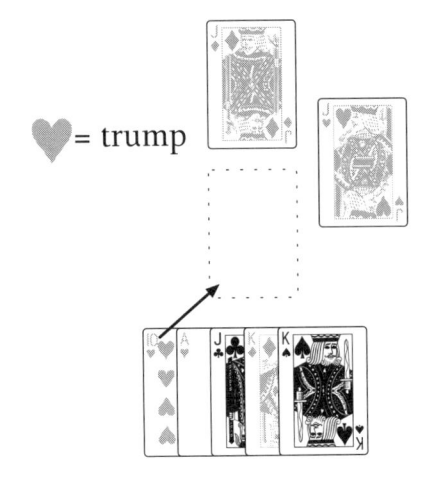

♥ = trump

Fig. 6: Using a backer

If your partner calls trump, play your Bowers right away (unless you'd be trumping your teammate's Ace!). This will allow your partner to strategize better and possibly win all five tricks.

As in other trick-taking games, always remember the highest unplayed card of each suit. In **Fig. 7**, for example, suppose you know that both Bowers have already been played. Your partner led with a King. As you don't have any Diamonds, you will have to play a trump. Should you play your King or 9? It is critical that you know whether the Ace of Trump is still unplayed. If the Ace is still unplayed, you can consider playing the 9 and saving your King for the final trick.

♣ = trump

Fig. 7: The highest unplayed card

GIN RUMMY

How the game evolved

In 1950, the United States Playing Card Co. conducted a survey of American cardplayers and discovered that the Rummy family of card games was our favorite family game. And why not? As David Parlett wrote in *The Penguin Book of Card Games*, "Rummy is deservedly popular because it is easy to learn, fast to play, suitable for all ages, playable by any number, and as suitable for gamblers as for missionaries—though perhaps not both at once." Gin Rummy is the most sophisticated member of the oldest branch of the Rummy family tree—the one in which the object is to be the first to "go out."

Three nations claim the credit for the invention of Rummy. The only thing they all agree on is the time period when the inventing took place: the 1800s. Let's start with...

The Mexicans

The Spanish brought the first playing cards to the New World. The Indians living in the Spanish colonies used these cards to develop their own games, including one called Conquian, from the Spanish "con quien" ("with whom," as in "With whom are you playing?") Perhaps Conquian was originally a partnership game.

Conquian's rules were similar to many of the Rummy games. The major difference was that Conquian was played with a Spanish pack of 40 cards—the 10, 9, and 8 of each suit were removed. The Mexicans inherited this pack from the Spanish, but they didn't inherit this game. The earliest mentions of Rummy in Spanish card-game books appear much later in the 20th century and are obviously borrowings from across the Atlantic. Even the Spanish name for Rummy—Ramy—is a Spanish corruption of the English word.

At some point in the 18th century, Conquian migrated north into Texas, where the Texans, with their usual flair for language, dubbed it Coon-Can or Conkin. There are reports of Conquian in gaming literature as far back as 1860, but when the game finally made it into the hallowed pages of *Hoyle*, it was as Coon-Can (*The Standard Hoyle*, 1887). The name Conquian didn't appear in *Hoyle* until a decade later (*Foster's Complete Hoyle*, 1897). Stewart Culin, a 19th-century curator of the Smithsonian Institution, reported in *Chess and Playing Cards* (1896) that Conquian was a favorite among the Apaches of the American Southwest.

The French

Most scholars have put their money on the Mexican theory, but some believe that Rummy is a descendant of Poker (see our chapter on Poker, page 93), which most probably originated with French settlers in Louisiana. The French theory is based on some likenesses between the two games and on the liquor allusions in Rummy and Gin Rummy.

1. *The likenesses.* Poker and Rummy are the most popular games based on making combinations rather than on taking tricks. (In the 1950s, we would have had to add Canasta to that sentence; in that decade the fad from Uruguay was even bigger than Bridge.)

Combinations in the Rum family are called "melds." As in Poker, melds are made of cards that match each other according to specific guidelines. In Rummy, a *group* is three or more cards of the same rank (Q-Q-Q); a *sequence* is three or more cards of the same suit (A-2-3-4 of Hearts). Note the resemblance to Poker hands. (However, unlike Poker, where each deal is a game within a game, in Rummy the play never stops. Also unlike Poker, in Rummy you're penalized for whatever cards you haven't grouped at the end of the game.)

2. *The liquor.* Most of the backers of Poker as the parent of Rummy claim that Rummy appeared in the 1890s as Rum Poker. The American card authority John Scarne claimed it was called Whisky Poker which later became Rum Poker. (Scarne claims Rum Poker became Rum at the turn of the century to clean the game up for families. Rum represented drinking, but Poker apparently represented something much worse!) There was also at this time a Gin Poker. "The origins of Rummy," Parlett wrote, "would therefore appear to be lost not so much in the mists of time as in the alcoholic haze of history."

There are two obstacles to the acceptance of the French/Poker theory. One is Whisky, Rum, and Gin Poker all had rules much like Conquian's, and Conquian was reported long before the other three. The other is Rummy's first appearance in print, in a 1905 *Hoyle*, was as "Rhum, or Rhummy," spellings that suggest a European influence rather than drinking. Parlett tracked down a German game of that era that used "rum" to mean "honors" and a Dutch game that used "roem" to mean "meld."

To further complicate the issue, the game had become Rum by 1912, but in a 1919 card book, it was referred to as Poker Rum.

The Chinese

Poker and Rummy are similar to two board games with Chinese roots, Dominoes and Mah Jongg, in that all four games are built on the principle of making combinations. Therefore, a Chinese claim for the legacy of Rummy is not at all far-fetched.

In 1891, a British traveler named W.H. Wilkinson transformed a Chinese card game called Khanhoo into a game with a 62-card pack. Wilkinson borrowed from the Chinese (or invented) many rules similar to Rummy's. British researcher Andrew Pennycook, in *The Book of Card Games* (1982), found another Chinese game from that period that's a close cousin: Kon Khin. Now *that* sounds intriguing. Coincidence? Or did the Mexicans get this game from the Chinese? How would the transfer have happened? Answers to these questions might never be found, so let's move on to something we *can* answer—how Gin Rummy entered the world.

The Gin Game

Elwood T. Baker was living in New York and tutoring the well-to-do in Whist at the Knickerbocker Whist Club in the first decade of this century. (Yes, apparently in those days and in that place, you could make a living teaching people to play cards.) Baker was growing bored with Rummy and, in seeking to speed the game up, invented Gin Rummy. (The game was named by his young son, who apparently knew a few things about adults and their recreational pursuits.)

Parlett didn't believe Baker thought up Gin Rummy; he claimed that the Whist tutor only fine-tuned the scoring and then launched the nationwide craze for the game after teaching it to his students (the way Edmond Hoyle launched Whist). But Parlett can't always be right, and he offered no other candidate as Gin Rummy's inventor, so as far as we're concerned Elwood T. Baker and his claim to fame can rest peacefully.

Gin Rummy declined in popularity in the 1920s when the card world was assaulted by Contract Bridge. It resurfaced in the 1940s when it was taken up by Hollywood celebrities (a long-running Broadway show of this time, *The Gin Game*, added fuel to the fire). In the 1950s, Gin Rummy was shoved aside by the mania for Canasta. Today the game remains popular, though it's not near the peak it occupied at the time of the USPCC survey in 1950.

The biggest game in sports

A variation of Conquian called "Panguingue" (pronounced "pahn-gheeng-ghee") or "Pan" is still played today. The chief feature of this game is the number of cards used; five to eight Spanish packs (200 to 320 cards)! As many as 16 players can be accommodated in one deal, though they'd have to possess considerable patience to get through this gargantuan game.

How the game is played

Gin Rummy is played by two people with the standard 52-card pack. The cards in each suit rank from the King (the highest) down to the Ace (the lowest). Each face card counts as 10, each Ace counts as one, and the other cards are their stated values.

Each player receives 10 cards in the deal. The first card always goes to the non-dealer. The rest of the pack is placed faced-down; this is the "stock." The top card of the stock is turned up and placed beside the stock. This is the "upcard."

The non-dealer begins play by taking the first upcard or refusing it; if the non-dealer refuses the upcard, the option of taking it or refusing it passes to the dealer. If the dealer also refuses, the non-dealer draws the top card of the stock.

From there, each player in turn draws a card, either the upcard or the top card of the stock, and then discards one card (the new upcard) face up on the previous discards.

The object of all this taking and discarding is to form your hand into matched sets (three or four cards of the same rank) or sequences (three or more cards in sequence in the same suit).

After drawing, and before discarding, a player may "knock" if his or her unmatched cards count 10 or less. The player who knocks lays down 10 cards, arranged in sets and with the unmatched cards segregated, then discards the eleventh card. If all 10 cards are matched, the player's count is zero, and he or she is said to "go gin."

If neither player has knocked by the time the 50th card has been drawn (and a following discard made), there is no score for either player for that particular deal.

The opponent of the player who knocked may "lay off" any of his or her unmatched cards that fit on the knocker's matched sets, thereby reducing his or her own count of unmatched cards.

If the knocker has the lower count in unmatched cards, he or she wins the difference between the two players' counts. Should the opponent have an equal or lesser count, the opponent is said to have "undercut" the knocker. The opponent then scores the difference (if any) in the counts, plus a bonus of 25 points. The knocker cannot be undercut if he or she has gone gin. A player who goes gin scores the opponent's count of unmatched cards, if any, plus a bonus of 25 .

The first player to accumulate 100 points wins the game. A 100-point bonus is added to the winner's score. Then each player adds 25 points to his or her total score for each hand won; this is called a "box" or "line" bonus. The winner wins the difference in total scores. If the loser did not score a point, this difference is doubled. A game like that is called a "shutout" or a "schneider," and the loser has been "skunked."

Strategies

Although gaining three sets almost always assures you a knock, the clock is ticking fast, and the hand may end before you're ready. The important thing is that you beat your opponent to the punch, knock first and take the points derived from the other player's deadwood. Make it your overall goal to form two sets and retain a mix of lower cards (adding up to 10 or less). This is the fastest means of knocking first. However, to get to this point, you should understand the difference between the early and late phases of the game and the different strategies required during each.

Fig. 1 shows a Gin Rummy game in the early phase (the opening deal). You have the option here of taking the 3 of Spades. This may appear to be a good choice as it gives you a combination pair, and it's a low card (low cards are better when counting deadwood). However, getting good combinations doesn't help that much because forming sets wins games of Gin Rummy. You should almost always draw from the stock, unless you can form a set or extend an existing set by taking the discard. In this case, you decide to draw, pulling an 8 of Clubs (**Fig. 2**).

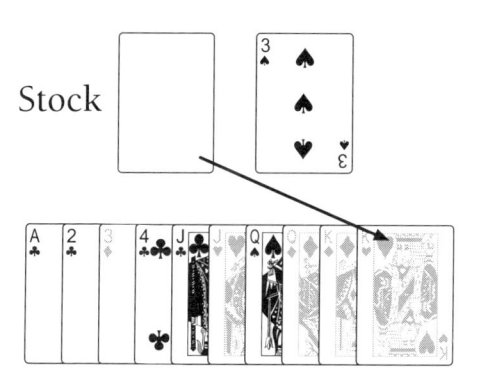

Fig. 1: Preferring the stock

The 8 of Clubs doesn't help your hand at all, and you discard it. In this situation, it's obvious that keeping your Jacks, Queens, and Kings is better than hanging onto the 8, because you have a pair of each. Even if you only had one King, you should probably keep that over the 8. Discarded face cards are very common, and your chances of matching a King via the discard pile are very high. For example, in this case your opponent is not likely to have a pair of Kings (since you have two) and will probably discard a single King, so it doesn't end up as deadwood in his or her hand.

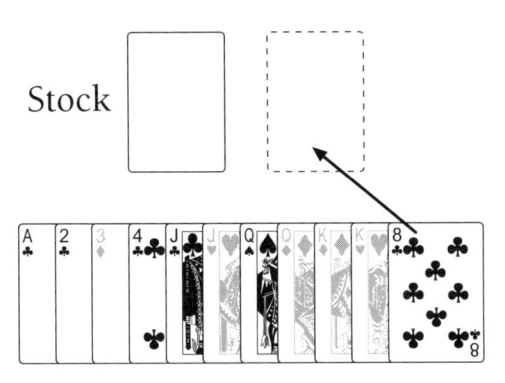

Fig. 2: Keeping face cards

Your opponent takes the 8 and, not unexpectedly, discards a face card—the Jack of Diamonds (**Fig. 3**). You snap it up to form a set of three Jacks. Now, your discard is more difficult. You have four very low cards and may want to hang onto them. However, with your low cards there is only one card that can complete a set, the 3 of Clubs. Since it will be much easier for you to form a set with higher cards, you throw away the 4 of Clubs.

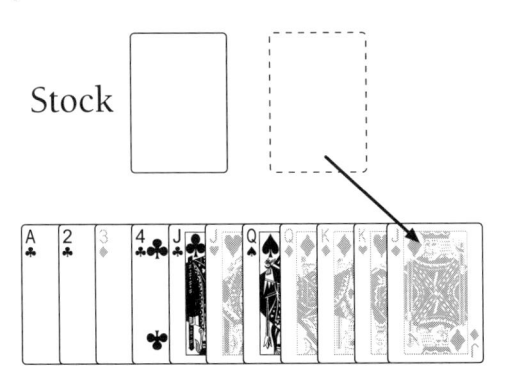

Fig. 3: Discarded face cards

Your opponent discards the 10 of Spades. This card wouldn't form a set, so you ignore it. You draw from the stock, taking up the 2 of Diamonds (**Fig. 4**). Now that the game has progressed several turns, you decide the time is right to rid your hand of Kings and Queens. Waiting up to six turns before getting rid of higher-ranking cards is normally an acceptable strategy, but with the 2 of Diamonds added to your hand, all your lower ranking cards are forming combinations, so you don't want to lose them. You dissolve your pair of Kings by discarding the King of Diamonds.

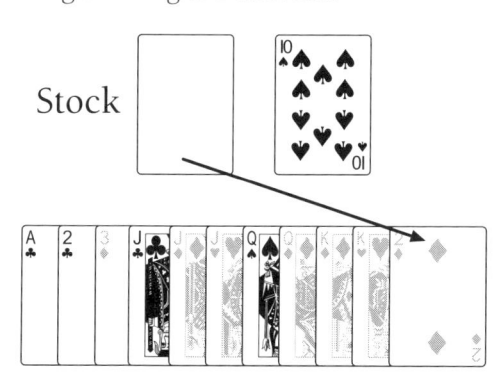

Fig. 4: Dissolving the higher pair

Your opponent discards another Jack, which you take into your hand, adding to your set. Your discard this turn is more obvious, and your useless King goes into the discard pile (**Fig. 5**). As an unmatched higher-ranking card, the King is now an encumbrance, and you should rid yourself of this excess baggage.

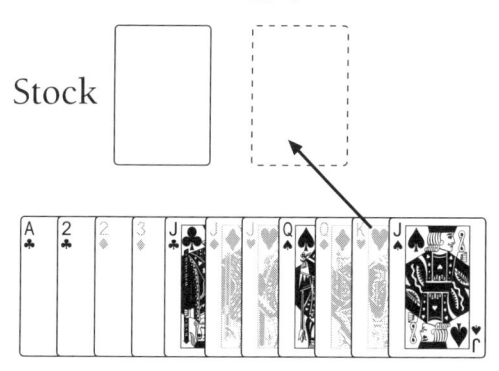

Fig. 5: Discarding unmatched higher cards

Hoyle® Card Games 75

Advanced Strategies

The sharper Gin Rummy players can track the discards to help them avoid discarding good cards to their opponents. It also enables them to hold onto the best card combinations. For example, take a look at **Fig. 6**. Here, you have drawn a 5 of Diamonds from the stock. To win the game, you need another set. Which of your card combinations are most likely to produce a set? Keeping the 5 and discarding the 8 seems prudent as the 5 and pair of 6s are a versatile combination. Suppose, however, that the 6 of Spades has already been buried in the discard pile? In this case, trying to get three 6s is futile. The only available 6 that completes the sequence is the 6 of Clubs, and this card is better matched to the 7 and 8 (doing so reduces your deadwood). You should dissolve the pair, and discard the 6 of Hearts.

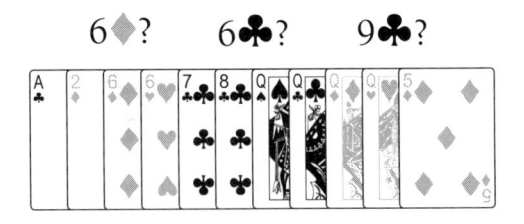

Fig. 6: Reading the discard pile

To add a further plot twist (and show you another use for remembering the discards), suppose your opponent picked up the 9 of Diamonds from the discard pile in the beginning of the game, and later threw out the 10 of Diamonds. This is a sign that your opponent is not attempting a Diamond sequence, but has a set of 9s instead. In this case, the 9 of Clubs is probably sitting cozily in your opponent's hand. The 7 and 8 in your hand are essentially worthless, and they displace the 6 of Hearts (since they're higher ranking) as the prime candidates for discard.

GO FISH

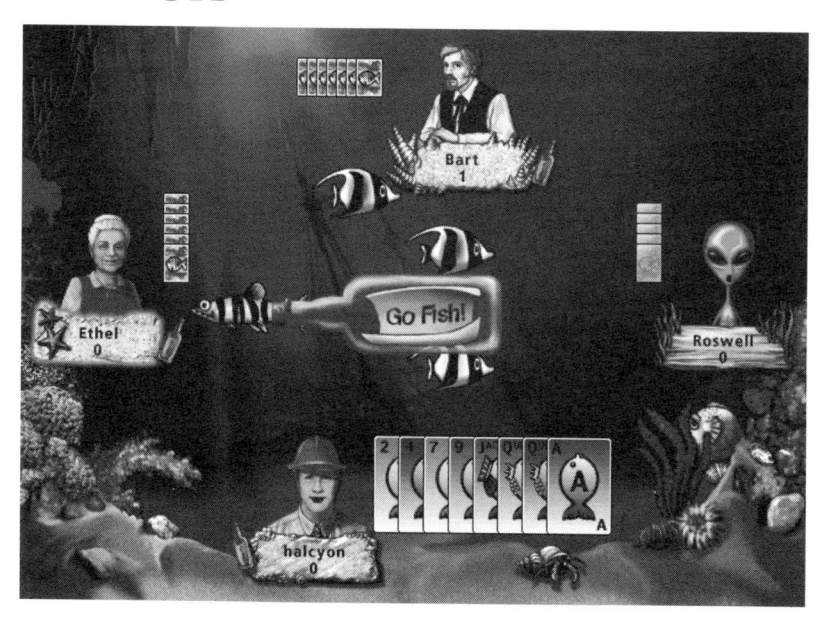

How the game evolved

Go Fish is perhaps the simplest representative of the family of "exchange to collect" card games, where the goal is to take cards from your opponents in order to make matching sets. (This is in contrast to the family of "exchange to scapegoat" games, like Old Maid, where the goal is to get your opponents to take certain cards from you.) Another important feature of Go Fish is that of matching cards in your hand to cards available from the table. This is referred to as "fishing" in China, where, according to *The Oxford Guide to Card Games*, such matching games are as popular as trick-taking games are in the west. The exception seems to be Italy, where the national games of Scopa and Scopone are of the fishing type. In fact, according to the game historian David Parlett, in the sixteenth century, a popular Italian gambling game was called Andare a Piscere (Go Fish).

How the game is played

Each player gets five cards. If you are dealt a four of a kind, or get four of a kind during game play, those cards are removed from your hand, and you get a point.

Moving clockwise, players take turns asking a specific player for a given rank of card. If someone asks you for a rank that you have, the cards are taken from your hand. if you do not have any cards of that rank, your opponent must "go fish," taking one new card from the pile of cards.

When it's your turn, select a player you think might have a needed card. Pick one card from your hand of the desired rank. If the player has the desired card, he or she must pass it over. If not, you must "go fish." If you get the card you asked for, you get to go again.

If you run out of cards and there are still cards left, you get five free cards.

Play continues until all hands are empty and there are no more cards to draw from. The winner is the player with the most points at the end of the game.

Strategies

Winning at Go Fish takes luck, a decent memory, and a good sense of timing. The luck part we can't help you with. Ditto for a decent memory (actually, you can read the strategies section in Memory Match for some mnemonic aids). Try to remember what people have asked for in previous turns. This is especially important if someone has captured two cards of a specific rank. If you have the opportunity to ask for that rank, make sure you take it—you'll get a warm feeling when you lay down four cards.

Timing refers to the best moment to risk everything, reveal your hand, and go for matches. This won't happen until the second half of the game. In the first half of the game, while most of the deck is in the stockpile, it is difficult to score points. You are better off hiding your hand from your opponents. Choose one or two cards in your hand, and keep asking other players for those cards every turn. When the stockpile gets low, most of the cards you need will now be sitting in the other players' hands. Start asking for cards, and keep asking. Often, the last three or four sets will be taken by one person, bringing the game to a sudden close.

HEARTS

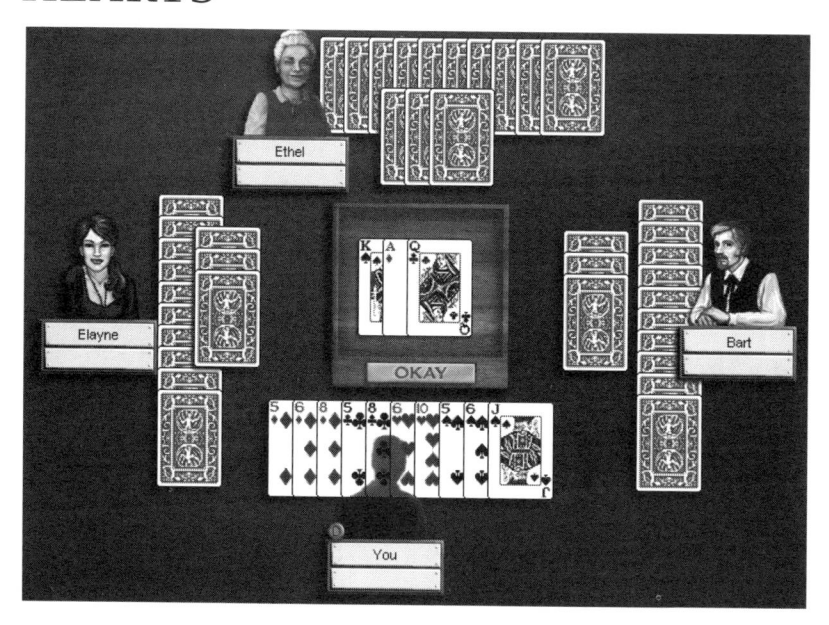

How the game evolved

The concept of turning games around and letting the losers win and the winners lose has been applied to most of the card-game families. It seems to work best with the family of trick-taking games. Hearts (also known as Omnibus Hearts, Black Maria, and Black Lady) is the most successful example of a trick-avoidance game. Merilyn Simonds Mohr noted its international reputation— the only game of its type to ascend to those heights. The United States Playing Card Co. reports that Hearts is the second-favorite card game among American college students (Spades is number one).

The first unmistakable sighting of the game was in an American book, *Trumps' New Card Games* (1886). So where did Hearts come from? The writer R.F. Foster asked this question of his readership in *Foster on Hearts* (1895). The response must have been dismal, because Foster doesn't elaborate on this subject in any of his many subsequent books on cards.

Though we can't pinpoint an evolutionary path for Hearts, we know it descends, however indirectly, from a French game called Reversis (first recorded in 1601). Reversis is probably the ancestor of all trick-avoidance games. According to David Parlett in *A History of*

Card Games, Reversis was sufficiently popular to warrant a book devoted to it as early as 1634, and it remained in most game manuals until late in the 1800s. Parlett, who cruised the pages of every *Gamester* and *Hoyle* of the past 300 years, said that despite this Whist-like longevity, Reversis never made much headway in the English-speaking countries.

This leaves us with the mystery of Hearts. Until the missing link in the evolutionary chain is found, we'll never know how this French game of the Renaissance became so popular in American college dormitories.

How the game is played

The usual number of Hearts players is four (three, five, and six may also play, but we won't consider those variants here). It's every man (or woman) for himself.

Hearts uses the standard 52-card pack. The cards in each suit rank from the Ace (the highest) to the 2 (the lowest). There are no trumps.

The deal rotates clockwise, as does the play of the cards. The entire pack is dealt, one card at a time. Players may discard three cards by passing them to the player on their left. (You must pass these cards before you can look at the ones you'll be receiving.) The player with the 2 of Clubs opens the game. In **Hoyle Card Games**, passing can rotate or be dispensed with, and the player to the dealer's left can open.

Whichever card is led first, the other players must try to follow suit. A trick is won by the highest card in the suit led. The winner of a trick makes the next lead.

The object of play is to avoid taking Hearts in tricks, as each Heart counts as one point against the player taking it. The Queen of Spades (the "Black Lady" or "Black Maria") counts as 13. However, you could try to take ALL the hearts AND the Black Lady. This is called "Shooting the Moon," and, if you pull it off, you hand your opponents a whopping 26 points each.

Hearts cannot be led until they've been "broken," that is, thrown into a previous trick by a player who couldn't follow suit.

When a player equals or breaks 100 points, the game is over, and the player with the lowest score at that time is the winner.

Strategies

The Queen of Spades rules the game of Hearts. To ignore the Queen is to court humiliation and risk defeat. Consideration of the Queen should begin before play starts, during the passing phase. Any high Spades (Q, K, A) are dangerous if they are not protected by several lower Spades. For example, if dealt the hand shown in **Fig. 1**, your Queen is almost unprotected (only the Jack helps). If you keep her, as shown in **Fig. 2**, you will most likely get stuck with her later during a trick.

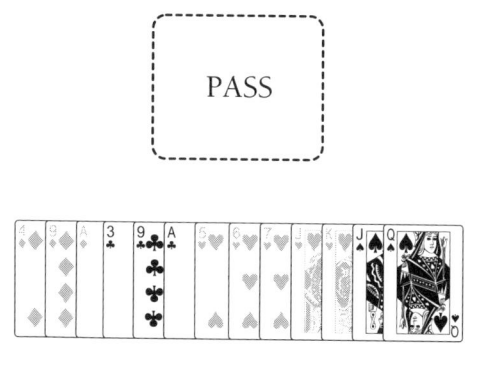

Fig. 1: Unprotected high Spade

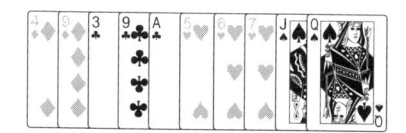

Fig. 2: Poor discard

Fig. 3 shows a different situation in which keeping the Queen is actually desirable. Here, with five Spades in your hand, you are almost guaranteed of passing off the Queen to someone else. You just need to wait for the right opportunity (discussed later).

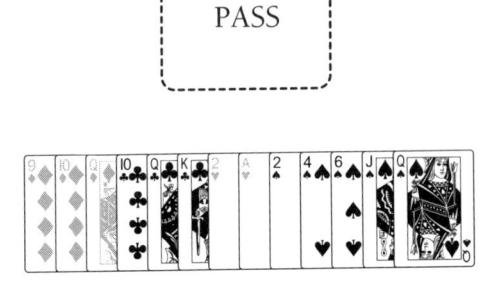

PASS

Fig. 3 Well-protected Queen

Don't be nervous about keeping high-cards in your hard. Keeping high-cards in combination with low cards is not usually dangerous. For example, **Fig. 4** shows the game in progress (3rd trick). You must play a Diamond. You can play the 2 or Ace. Play your Ace, and save the 2. This early in the game, it is unlikely you'll take a heart. The last player probably still has a Diamond. It's a harmless trick, and you won't score points.

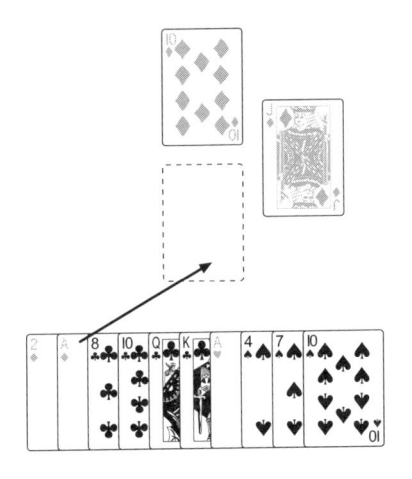

Fig. 4: Playing the high cards

However, it can be fatal to be short on low cards in a particular suit, especially later in the game. Continuing the previous example, let's say a few hands have passed, and you still have the 8, 10, Queen, and King of Clubs (**Fig. 5**). After the Ace and 9 are played, you happily throw down your Queen, and the top player takes the trick with the Ace. However, the player to your right threw down the Jack of Clubs. You now have the three highest Clubs (8, 10, K).

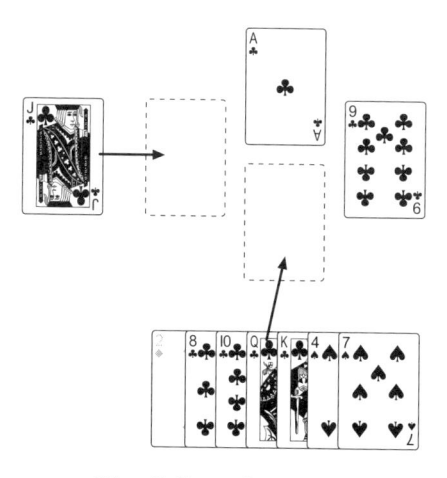

Fig. 5: Long in a suit

What happens after that could be destructive. Players will be running out of Clubs, and next time someone leads in Clubs, they'll paint you in red with Hearts or stick you with the Queen of Spades (**Fig. 6**).

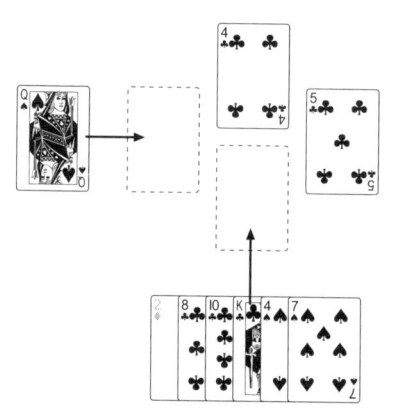

Fig. 6: Running out of options

Hoyle® Card Games

Guarded high-cards should be saved until later in the game, especially if they are Hearts. This will help to prevent someone from successfully Shooting the Moon. If the player who receives your discards likes to Shoot the Moon, you may wish to pass them a low Heart. This may discourage them from making the attempt in the first place.

MEMORY MATCH

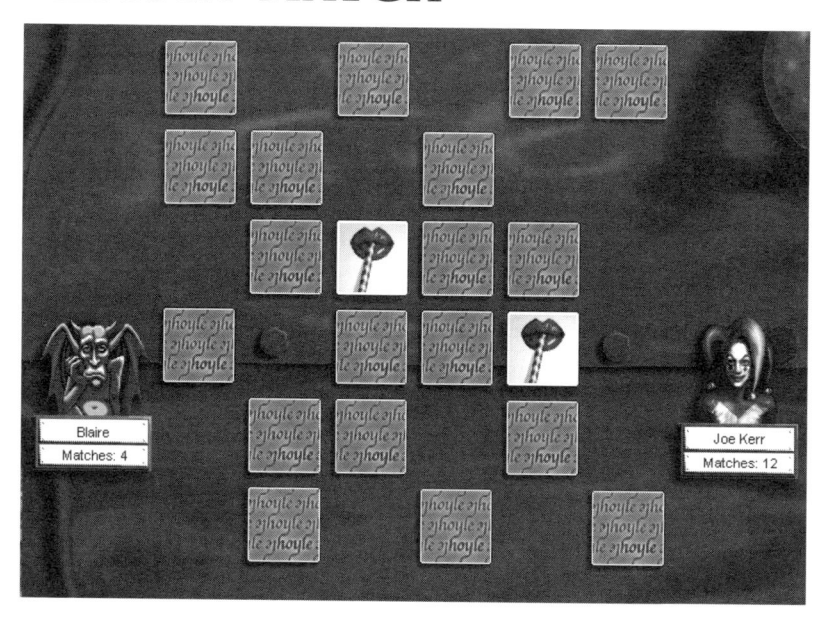

How the game evolved

Just as the Olympic games are tests of basic human physical abilities, pushed to their extremes, Memory Match is an extreme test of a basic human mental ability—remembering. Surely simple games based on memorization are at least as old as the ancient Olympics. And just as in the Olympics there is the important distinction between sprints and marathons, there are different types of memory that can be exercised: short-term and long-term. Short-term memory is not usually as reliable as we would like (just ask someone who can't remember anyone's name at a party). Remembering unrelated bits of information quickly is quite a challenge for people and has made for the invention of many simple but entertaining memory games.

Systematic research into human memory is a relatively new field. Although they are now terms of common parlance, the words "short-term" and "long-term" memory have only been used in the latter half of the twentieth century. Psychological studies have helped to define what short-term memory is, and have also suggested techniques for helping people improve their short-term memory. It is generally agreed, for instance, that on average people can remember about seven independent pieces of information for about thirty seconds.

Remembering more things requires practicing techniques for "chunking" multiple pieces of information into one, thus making better use of those "seven pieces." Remembering for longer periods requires transferring information from short-term memory into long-term memory. How this happens is certainly a complicated mental process, but, as anyone knows who has memorized a poem or a speech, repetition and practice seem to be the key.

Practical methods for improving short-term memory go back farther than the term itself. At the turn of the century, the Pelman Institute in Britain devised a number of techniques for helping people improve their memory. A legacy of this is that the game we call Memory Match is referred to in England as "Pelmanism."

How the game is played

Cards are dealt face down into a grid layout. The object of the game is to find and remove all matching pairs of cards. Click on a card to turn it over, then click a second card. If the two cards are a pair, they are removed from the layout. If not, they are turned face down.

—If you find three pairs in a row without a miss, you get a bonus.

—If you turn over a wild card and any non-wild card, the wild card and both the non-wild card and its pair are all removed from the layout.

—When all pairs have been found and the board is empty, your score is displayed. Matched pairs, misses, bonuses, layout size, and deck difficulty all affect your score (choose "Getting Started" from the Game menu and go to the Scoring tab for more details).

—Go to "Settings" (Game menu) to change the number of cards in the layout and level of difficulty of the deck.

Strategies

Save your best efforts for your first few games. After that, unless you've had too much coffee, your brain begins throbbing and card positions from earlier games begin blending in your mind.

You can make your selections by following a pattern (e.g., top to bottom). This may help you to remember card positions. On the other hand, if you're playing head to head, you might want to avoid patterns, lest you inadvertently help your opponent more than yourself.

Advanced techniques have been devised that can turn otherwise normal human beings into Johnny Mnemonics. We will only mention a few here:

Naming: If you start giving permanent names to pictures (e.g., you name the female Greek image Aphrodite), it might help you remember the image.

Visualization: You can lock an item into your memory through visualization and association. The visualization part is easy since we are dealing with images. For example, if the spiderweb card shows up in a corner, remember this: cobweb corner (the alliteration of "c-c" also helps!). As another example, the card with lips can become "lower lips" or "upper lips" depending on its location.

Chaining: This method uses visualization, but links several items together. For example, if you turned over a row of cards depicting the Greek statue, flies, and a doughnut, you could remember it this way: "Aphrodite is bothered by flies that like doughnuts."

Use an Acrostic: A phrase or word derived from the first letter of other words is called an acrostic. For example, SAIDRO can be used to describe a row of these six cards: Symbol, Aphrodite, Insect, Doughnut, Rat, Old (woman).

As a final tip for the more casual gamers, if you think you might know the location of a pair, ALWAYS turn the card you're least sure about first. This method is definitely less embarrassing if you're wrong.

OLD MAID

How the game evolved

Old Maid is part of a family of basic card games in which the mechanisms of play are as simple as possible. The simplest mechanism of all is that of exchanging cards with other players. One subfamily of exchange games is the negative or "scapegoat" group; in these games, holding the scapegoat card at the end of the hand brings with it a penalty, from loss of points to loss of the game. The best-known negative game in English is Old Maid (for which we have exactly zero evolutionary data).

The flipside of these negative games, those in which collecting rather than discarding cards is the object, include the Rummy family and the children's game Go Fish.

Old Maid can be played with a standard deck of cards by removing all but one of a particular card to be the Old Maid; typically a Queen.

Hoyle Card Games uses a special animal deck containing ten different animal ranks (as opposed to 13), and one Troll card that serves as the Old Maid.

How the game is played

After the cards are dealt, each player discards, face-up, all of his or her pairs (never three or four of a kind). Then each player, on his or her turn, draws one card from the face-down hand of the player on his or her right.

If the drawn card makes a pair with a card in his or her hand, that player removes the pair. The player to the left then draws one card from the player on his or her right, and so on.

Eventually one player will be left with the troll, the "Old Maid." That ends the game, and the possessor of the Old Maid is the loser.

PINOCHLE

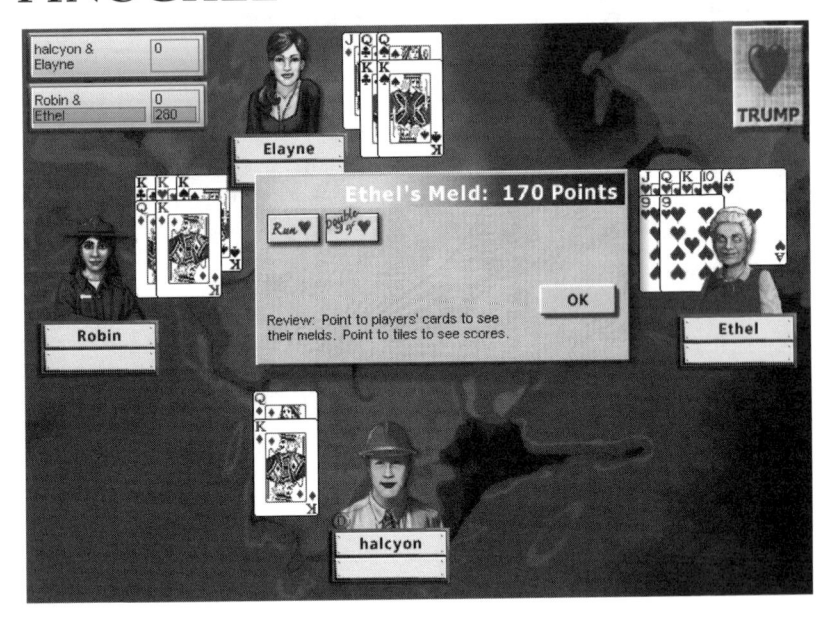

How the game evolved

Pinochle is derived from several different card game traditions. The oldest of its traditional features are the Ace-10 hierarchy and marriages. Ace-10 games, in which 10s supercede Kings in worth and power, probably were combined with marriage games at some point in the early 18th century. A marriage game refers to any card game that includes point-scoring opportunities arrived at by matching the King and Queen of the same suit. Also related to the marriage concept is the joining of the Jack of Diamonds to the Queen of Spades (called Pinochle).

The marriage element preceded all other elements. Queens did not exist as card figures until the 15th century in Germany. They first showed up in a game called "Poch." Not long after that a French game, "Glic," included marriages as a scoring combination. Poch and Glic are also the early ancestors of modern Poker.

"Sixty-Six" and "Binokel," two German games in the Ace-10 category, had by the early 18th century acquired the trick-taking format common to several other games. Shortly thereafter, a game called "Mariagen-Spiel," shortened to "Mariage," appeared in Germany. Its French name is misleading, a result of the fact that throughout Europe the nobility spoke French rather than their native tongues. Mariage was probably a German creation of the upper class.

From there the story shifts to France. Paris casinos in the 1840s were surprised by the sudden appearance of "Bezique," a game that included the Ace-10 feature, marriages, and an interesting scoring phenomenon that paired up Jacks and Queens. Bezique was played in a double-pack of 64 cards ranking from Ace-7. Games were to 1,000 points.

In Bezique, the Queen of Spades could be matched to the Jack of Diamonds for points. These and other features apparently originated in an old French province named Limousin. The Spade Queen and her erstwhile companion invite considerable speculation. "Diamond Jack" is often viewed as a rogue; in some traditional games he is used as a joker or fool. His joining up with the Queen may be viewed as the herculean jest of card games.

Another interpretation is that the Jack of Diamonds represents Hector de Maris, a knight of the round table and half-brother of Lancelot. The Jack of Clubs is said to represent Lancelot himself. This leads to an easy guess that the two knights' face card identities were switched, and Lancelot's transgression with Queen Guinevere was mistakenly assigned to Hector. The whole matter would be clarified if it were possible to link that mythical lady to the Queen of Spades. Unfortunately, no such evidence exists.

At any rate, Bezique crossed the Atlantic and appeared in the *Modern Pocket Hoyle* in 1868. "Penuchle," however did not appear in *Hoyle* until 12 years later. The name and play was actually derived from Binokel (two-eyes), another German card game variation, and a cousin to Bezique. Binokel is played using the familiar 48-card pack (stripped of the 7s and 8s used in Bezique). The word binokel (or pince-nez) is probably another reference to the Jack and Queen. These two figures, cast in profile on most decks, have only one eye each. When you lay the two cards together, their single eyes combine as two eyes, and thus, binokel.

The precise spelling of Penuchle was contested for many years. An important junction occurred in 1907. In that year, R.H. Foster published *Complete Pinocle* and included a derogatory remark about the 'h' that others used when spelling the name. In 1908, he wrote another book, titled *Laws of Pocket Pinochle*. What happened to bring about this change of mind in Foster between 1907 and 1908 is most likely interesting, but also undocumented.

Penuchle and its predecessors had been two-handed games until the arrival of Rummy. Versions of Pinochle for three or more players quickly appeared to stave off the Rummy threat. In the decades since then, Pinochle became one of America's most popular card games.

How the game is played

Partnership Auction Pinochle is played with one 48-card deck of Pinochle cards and four players are grouped in teams of two. The players sitting opposite each other are partners. It is conventional to name the players North, South, East, and West. North and South are partners, as are East and West.

Each player receives 12 cards. The deck contains 12 cards in each of four suits—two in each of the ranks Ace, 10, King, Queen, Jack, and 9. The rank of cards differs from normal custom—the 10 outranks everything (within its suit) except the Ace.

Bid: The winner of the bid has the right to name the trump suit and gets to play the first trick. The minimum opening bid is 100 points, and the player to the dealer's left starts the bidding. Bids are made in multiples of 10 points. Each player must either bid at least 10 points higher than the previous bid or pass. When only one person has not said "pass," that person has won the bid. After the bidding is over, each player has the opportunity to meld.

Meld: There are three types of melds, and a card may belong to different melds as long as they are of different types. Each player places face-up on the table only those cards being melded.

Sequences

A, 10, K, Q, J of the trump suit (Run) 150
K,Q in Trump (Royal Marriage) 40
K,Q of any other suit (Common Marriage) 20

Special

One Jack of Diamonds and one Queen of Spades
(Pinochle) 40

Both Jacks of Diamonds and both Queens of Spades
(Double Pinochle) 300

9 of Trump (called the dix, pronounced "deece") 10

Groups

One Ace in each suit (Aces around) 100

One King in each suit (Kings around) 80

One Queen in each suit (Queens around) 60

One Jack in each suit (Jacks around) 40

The partners' separate melds are added into one total, but the team does not actually receive the meld points until they win a trick.

The Play (Taking Tricks)

All players pick up their meld cards, and the bid winner plays the opening lead. Proceeding to the left, each player plays a card on the trick following these rules:

—If a player has a card of the same suit as the lead card, it must be played. If possible, the player must play a card with a higher rank than the card that currently controls the trick.

—If a player has no cards in the suit led, a trump must be played if possible. If the trick already contains trump, the player must beat it with a higher trump if possible.

—If a player cannot follow suit and cannot play a trump, any other card may be played.

—If someone has already trumped, later players who can follow suit may play any card of the suit led, because no card of the led suit can beat a trump.

The highest trump wins the trick. If no trump was played, the highest-ranking card of the suit led wins the trick. If there is a tie for highest-ranking card, the trick is won by whichever of the equal cards was played first. The trick winner leads to the next trick, and so on until all 12 tricks have been played.

In the trick-taking phase of the game, the Aces, 10s, and Kings are worth 10 points each, and so are called "counters." Queens, Jacks, and 9s are not worth points (although they can win tricks); thus they are called "non-counters." The team that wins the final trick gets an additional 10 points.

Scoring: Each side adds up the points it won in tricks and adds the points from its melds (if it has won at least one trick). Bidder's opponents add their total into the accumulated score. If the bidder's team wins at least the amount of the bid, they add the amount won to the accumulated score.

If they don't make the bid, they subtract the bid from their accumulated score.

The side that first reaches 1,000 points wins a game.

Doublepack

This version of Pinochle uses a larger deck (80 cards), which allows for a greater scoring potential in the melds (see the online help for a Doublepack scoring table). There are no 9s in the Doublepack deck. Each player is dealt 20 cards to start. 3,550 points are needed for a win.

Partnership Pinochle

This game is like Partnership Auction, but there is no bidding. The last card is dealt face up and sets Trump. Players (taking turns starting left of the dealer) can exchange the 9 of Trump for the upcard, and receive 10 points for doing so. After this, the dealer takes the original or exchanged upcard. If the original upcard is a 9, the dealer picks it up for 10 points. However, the dealer cannot meld the 9 in this case.

Four-Handed Pinochle

This game is like Partnership Pinochle, but there are four individual players and no teams.

Two-Handed Pinochle

This two player Pinochle game is quite different from the others. The object of the game is to win tricks and subsequently meld certain combination of cards that have a scoring value. The deck is a standard 48-card Pinochle deck.

Each player receives 12 cards, non-dealer first. The next card is turned up and placed on the table; it is the trump card and determines the trump suit. The remainder of the pack, the stock, is placed face down.

The non-dealer leads the first trick. If a trump is led, it wins the trick unless the opponent plays a higher trump. If any other suit is led, the card led wins unless the opponent plays a higher card of the same suit or a trump. The leader may play any card, and the follower may play any card; there is no requirement to follow suit or to play a higher card to win the trick. The trick winner then has the option of melding. After each trick, both players draw a card from the top of the stock to restore their hands to 12 cards with the trick winner drawing first. The trick winner leads the next trick.

Upon winning a trick, and before drawing from the stock, a player may meld any combination of cards having value (see Partnership Auction Pinochle melds above). The meld is formed by placing the cards face up, where they remain until played in a trick or until the stock has been emptied.

Melding is subject to the following restrictions:

1. Only one meld may be made in a turn.
2. For each meld, at least one card must be taken from the hand and placed on the table.

A card once melded may be melded again only in a different class, or in a higher-scoring meld of the same class. If a player has melded a Royal Marriage and later adds the Ace, 10, and Jack of Trumps for a run, he scores an additional 150 points. If a player has melded a Pinochle and later adds another Pinochle for a Double Pinochle, the player only scores an additional 260 points, instead of 300. (If the first Pinochle had already been broken up, only 40 points would be scored for the second one.)

If a player has won a trick and has the dix (9 of Trump), the player may do one of the following:

1. Score 10 points by exchanging the trump card for his dix (dix trade) if no player has already done a dix trade.
2. Meld the dix for 10 points and lose the chance to do a dix trade with that card.

The winner of the 12th trick, after a possible final meld, draws the last card of the stock, which is shown to the opponent. The opponent draws the trump card (or the dix, if an exchange has been made). Each player picks up any meld cards on the table put them back in their hands. The winner of the 12th trick now leads and the rules of the play for the final 12 tricks are as follows:

1. The follower must follow the suit to the card led, if able.
2. The follower must try to win the trick by playing a higher card of the suit led, or by trumping, if able.
3. There is no melding during the last 12 tricks.

Melds are scored when they are made. Scores for cards taken in tricks are added to each player's score as the tricks are won. A player receives 11 points for each Ace, 10 points for each 10, four points for each King, three points for each Queen, and two points for each Jack taken in tricks. The player who win the last trick gets a 10-point bonus. The player who reaches 1,000 points first wins the game.

Strategies

As in most bidding games, it is important in Pinochle (Partnership Auction and Doublepack) not to overbid. The cost of overbidding is high; you lose all points gained during the current round, plus your bid is subtracted from your score.

To avoid underbidding and overbidding, estimate your bid by evaluating the worth of your hand. The traditional method of evaluating your hand assigns the following values to your cards:

Ace = 20 points

10 = 10 points

Each trump over three cards = 20 points

Meld = additional points

Fig. 1 shows a hand that you can expect to score 190 points. The two Aces are worth 40 points, and the 10 is worth 10 (50 points total). If you win the bid, you'll declare Hearts as trump; your fourth, fifth, and sixth trump equal 60 points (110 total). Next, you count your meld points. Your 9 of Hearts is worth 10 as dix (120 total). You have one royal marriage worth 40 (150 total) and one Pinochle worth 40 points (190 total).

Fig. 1: Evaluating your hand

Don't hesitate to bid the full value of your hand. It will allow you to choose trump, which empowers your hand during play (particularly when you're long in one suit).

When melding begins, look for marriages first, because they're the easiest to spot. The Jack of Diamonds and the Queen of Spades (forming Pinochle) are a slippery pair and can be hard to see—make sure you're thorough when looking for points.

Winning at Pinochle is a team effort. If it appears that your partner will win the trick, play a "counter" (King, 10, or Ace) to boost your score. The Ace is your only usual exception to this; only play an Ace as a counter if it's not a winner anymore (e.g., the suit has led three times). **Fig. 2** shows an example of playing counters. In this example, both Aces have been played, and the player on the left is not expected to trump. Your partner has played a 10 and is likely to win the trick (the player on the right has played the lesser-valued Queen). To give your team an extra 10 points, you should play the King of Diamonds.

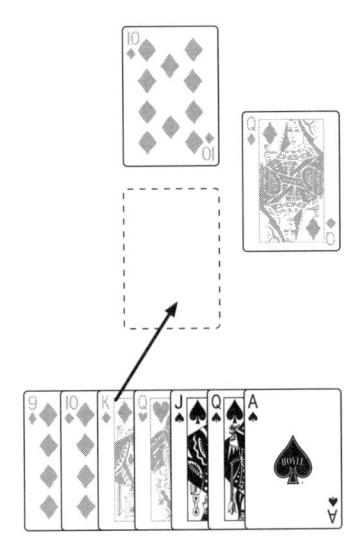

Fig. 2: Playing "counters"

Conversely, if your opponent is going to win the trick, throw a "non-counter" (**Fig. 3**). In this case, either the Jack or Queen of Spades should be played, rather than the Ace.

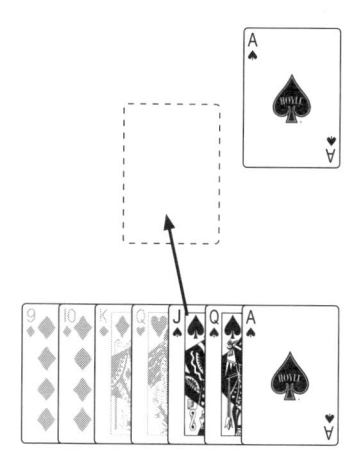

Fig. 3: Playing a "non-counter"

If you're leading, you can play a Queen to force your opponents to play counters. This strategy is made even more effective if you think your partner will win the trick.

Advanced Strategies

A sharp player of Pinochle demonstrates "multi-tasking" skills. You have to think about your best card to play while keeping track of what has been previously played. The good news is a photographic memory is not required, and you don't have to remember every single card! The two most important factors are: 1) What is the highest unplayed card in each suit? and 2) What suits are the other players void in?

Fig. 4 shows that the player on the right has led with the Jack of Clubs. The end of the hand is approaching fast. Your King beats the Jack, but should you play it? Suppose you've seen both 10s of Clubs, but neither Ace of Clubs. You know the highest unplayed Clubs are the two Aces. Your opponent on the left most likely has at least one of them. If you play the King, you'll give away a counter while losing the trick. It's better to hold off.

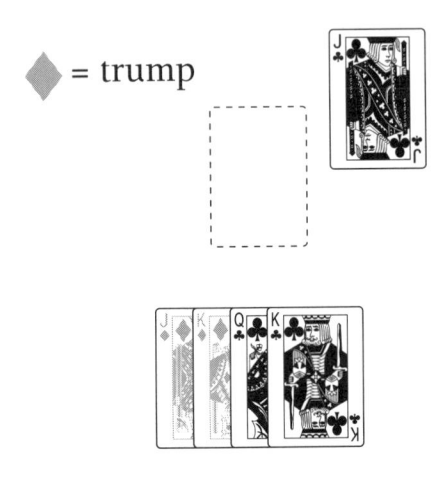

◆ = trump

Fig. 4: Highest unplayed card

As another example, with the cards shown in **Fig. 5**, you decide to lead with the 9 of Spades, a sure loser. You choose the 9 because you know both Aces of Spades are still unplayed. Playing the 9 is much better than playing your highest card (the 10 of Spades). Your 10 is a loser right now; the chances are 1 in 2 that the next player has an Ace of Spades.

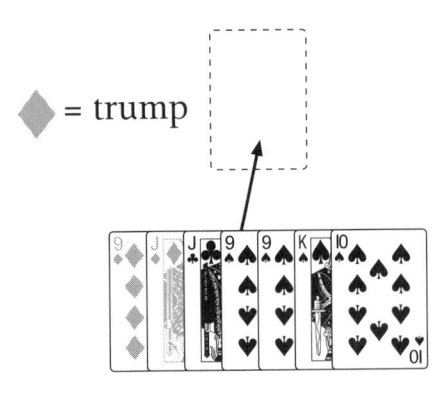

◆ = trump

Fig. 5: Highest unplayed card (II)

Suppose the player on the left surprises you and doesn't have the Ace, and trumps your 9 (**Fig. 6**). This means this player is void in Clubs, and you can file this information away for future use.

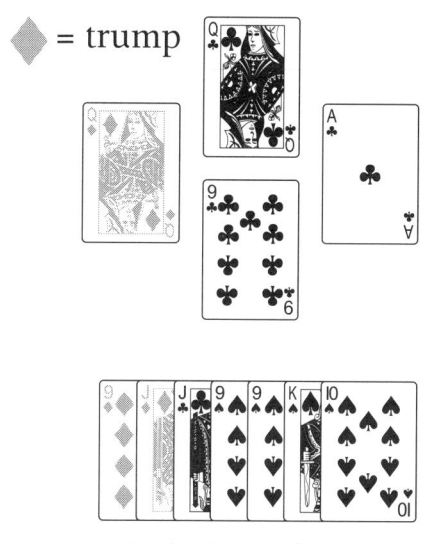

♦ = trump

Fig. 6: Trumped

An example of how this information can be useful occurs a few tricks down the road. If your partner (with the hand shown in **Fig. 7**) is leading, he or she may consider playing the Ace of Clubs. However, recalling that an opposing player is void in Clubs, your partner can avoid being trumped by playing something in another suit (the Jack or Queen of Diamonds).

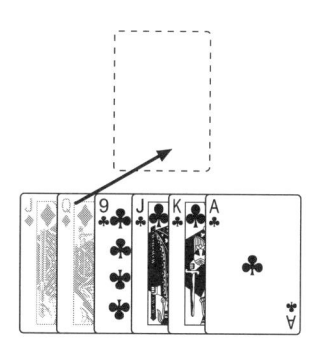

Fig. 7: Opponent void in Clubs

Of course, if you know your partner is void in a particular suit, you will want to play that suit, so your partner can play a trump. Sometimes, however, you may want to lead into the next player's void suit, so your partner can play a loser (since he or she doesn't have to beat the trick).

Strategies for Two-Handed Pinochle

This version of Pinochle is very different from the others. A meld occurs only after each trick and is carried out only by the winner of the trick. During the first 12 tricks, melding is crucial.

You want to play cards that won't be as valuable in melds. Remember that you don't have to follow suit for the first 12 tricks. 10s, 9s (but not 9 of Trump), and Jacks (but not the Jack of Diamonds) are your most expendable cards. Use 10s to win tricks when you're ready to meld. As usual, try to keep track of played cards. If both Queens of Spades have been played, for example, your Jack of Diamonds is worth little.

Cards that have already been melded can't be used again in a similar type of meld. For this reason, try to play these cards before your other cards. For example, in **Fig. 8** you have already scored the Queen of Spades for Pinochle and a Marriage. You would have to have four Queens to meld with her again. If this is unlikely, she is very expendable.

Fig. 8: Playing meld cards

It is important to win tricks just before the stock is emptied. You'll want to carry out any last melds you have while preventing your opponent from doing the same.

During the last 12 tricks, you should play your Aces before your opponent starts running out of suits. If you wish to force out your opponent's trump cards, play your long suits first. You may wish to do this if he or she has a lot of high trumps.

PITCH

How the game evolved

Pitch (also sometimes known as Setback or High-Low-Jack) is the most popular of a number of similar games originating from the game All Fours, a seventeenth-century English game. The name All Fours is a reference to the four points players try to take: High, Low, Jack and Game. The goal of all fours is to take "all four" of these points. The original All Fours incorporates some of Euchre's elements, including offering a turned up suit as trump.

Many variants of All Fours, including Pitch, Pedro, Seven Up, Cinch, Smear, and All Fives, cropped up in nineteenth century America. Most of these games include different styles of bidding and point values. In Pedro, for instance, you try to catch the 10 of trump instead of the game point.

There are versions of this game for two to seven players, but most commonly it is played by four players, with or without partnerships. The non-partnership version used in Hoyle Card Games is sometimes known as Cutthroat Pitch (probably because players gang up on the bidder, known as the "pitcher").

How the game is played

Pitch is a trick-taking game using a standard 52-card deck; each player is dealt six cards. Each player can bid on the value of his or her hand and plays to take tricks and get points. Although one player wins the bid and tries to take all the points, all players can get points by taking key cards. The goal is to be the first player to reach the winning score (7, 11, or 21).

Bidding

You can bid on the value of your hand. Possible bids are two, three, four, or smudge (smudge is really a bid of five).

For two, three, and four, you are bidding how many of the points below you can win. For smudge, you have to win all the points below, and take all six tricks in the round.

High You win the trick which has the highest available card in the trump suit.

Low You win the trick which has the lowest available card in the trump suit.

Jack You win the trick which has the Jack of the trump suit.

Game You get the most game points in the round. All 10s are worth 10, Aces are worth 4, Kings are worth 3, Queens are worth 2, and Jacks are worth 1. Other cards aren't worth anything.

Each player in turn bids or passes; bidding always starts at two. Bidding only lasts one round (each player only gets one chance to bid or pass). If all players pass, the cards are redealt and bidding starts again.

Note that since not all cards are dealt every hand, Ace and two aren't always the high and low card (sometimes a Queen may be the High and a four the Low, for instance). And there may not be a Jack in any given hand (since only 24 of 52 cards are dealt in a hand).

Scoring points

All points scored go to the player who scored them, but the pitcher must try to get the points he or she bid.

If you are the pitcher, and you win your bid, you get the number of points you took, even if this is higher than the bid. For instance, if you bid 2, and took High, Low, and Jack, that player gets 3.

But if you lose your bid, you are "set back" (you lose) the number of points you bid, even if you made some of the bid. For instance, if you bid 3, and get High and Low (but not Jack or Game), you lose 3, since you did not make all of your bid. If other players get the points you bid, they score those points. In this example, if another player got Jack and Game, he would get 2 points.

It is possible for two or more players to tie for Game (both receiving the same amount of total game points); in this case, no player gets that point. And again, if there is no Jack dealt, no one gets the Jack point.

Note that you must bid smudge to get the fifth point for winning smudge. Merely getting all six tricks and High, Low, Jack, and Game will still only give you 4 points if you didn't bid Smudge. If you bid Smudge, you must get all 4 points and win all the tricks, or you lose 5 points.

Bids are always scored in the order High, Low, Jack, and Game. Scoring stops when one player reaches the winning score. (This breaks any ties in the game.) For example: in a game played to a winning score of 11, Gax has 9 points and Roswell has 10 points. If Gax wins High and Low, and Roswell wins Jack and Game, Gax wins the game, because Gax gets 2 points for High and Low, making 11, and Roswell thus never gets his 2 points for Jack and Game. (This means in a close game, the person who's behind can win if he or she wins the right bids.)

Taking tricks

The player who won the bid (called the pitcher) plays a card to the board; the suit of this card is used as trump.

Each player must play trump if he or she has it (trump is shown in the upper right corner). The player with the highest trump card wins.

The player who won the first trick leads the next trick with any card. Each player, in turn, plays a card. If you have a card of the suit led, you must either follow suit or play a trump card. If you don't have a card of the suit led, you can play any card (trump, or any other suit).

Important! In Pitch, you can always choose to play trump, even if you can follow suit. If you don't have a card in the suit played, you can play any card, including trump.

The trick is won by the player who played the highest trump card, or, if there's no trump, the player who played the highest card of the suit that was led. The winner of each trick leads the next trick, and may lead any card.

Strategies

Bid based on the strong cards in your starting hand. If you have the Ace and a two or three, a bid of 2 is a strong bet. If you have an Ace and King, and other high cards, try bidding 4. And an Ace, King, and two is an excellent bid of 3.

Be careful about bidding based on holding a Jack, unless you have other cards in that suit to protect it (ideally higher cards); there's no guarantee you'll keep a Jack in your hand if you don't have supporting cards—and someone else is likely to get that point.

Watch out for your tens! Tens are worth a lot of points towards the Game bid, so be careful you don't give them away too easily. If you know you're likely to lose a trick (because it's been trumped or an Ace has been played), you might want to sacrifice a face card instead of a ten.

POKER

How the game evolved

Joseph Strutt was an 18th-century Englishman with a serious interest in fun. In 1801, he published the first book to investigate the origins of the games people play. Writing of a card game called "Primero," he described it as the oldest card game in England. Strutt wasn't much on aesthetic judgments (in the same book he said that Dominoes "could have nothing but the novelty to recommend it to the notice of grown persons in this country"), but he'd done his homework on Primero. Shakespeare played it. So did Henry VIII, when he wasn't marrying or imprisoning his wives. And what they were playing in Primero was the forerunner of the game we call Poker.

Primero (Primera in Spain; the English probably learned this game from the Spanish) was a three-card game (three cards were dealt to each player) that involved building cards into three kinds of hands, or combinations: three of a kind, pairs, and "fluxes" (our flush). Primero relied heavily on bluffing, and it attracted people who liked to gamble with cards.

By the 1700s, Primero had become a five-card game and had spread across Europe. It was now called "Brag" in England, "Pochen" in Germany, and "Poque" in France. Each game followed its own rules, though each retained the concepts of building combinations and bluffing.

The Mississippi River, mother of Poker

In the 18th century, Poque came to North America with the French colonists in what is now Louisiana. When President Thomas Jefferson purchased the Louisiana Territory in 1803, he couldn't have imagined he was buying America's national card game along with millions of acres of land.

In 1803, only the French around New Orleans were playing Poque, which used a short pack of 20 cards. (We don't know which cards were discarded, as the specific rules for Poque have not come down to us; we do know that the flux or flush of Primera was not part of Poque.) By the time of Jefferson's death in 1826, Poque was being played aboard a new invention, the steamboat, that was turning the Mississippi into America's first superhighway. By 1829 (60 years after the death of Edmond Hoyle), Americans had transformed Poque's name to Poker and expanded its deck to the full 52 cards.

Poker grew strong on the Mississippi, then rapidly moved west and east. What accounts for Poker's quick acceptance in America? Aside from the intrinsic qualities of the game, the prime reason might lie with the glamour of the American West. Americans have always romanticized the frontier; it's no accident that Westerns are a major genre in movies, literature, and television. The frontier, people believed, was a place where you could reinvent yourself on a larger and more successful scale, a place where you could live life more intensely than in Boston, Philadelphia, or Savannah. Everything Western has at one time or another been imitated elsewhere in the country, including Western amusements. If you couldn't ride a buckin' bronc or attend a necktie party in the ever-so-refined East, you could always play Poker.

Face-down versus face-up

Poque was first called Straight Poker or Cold Poker. All cards were dealt face-down, and there was only one round of betting.

Then the Americans went to work on it. By 1865, the end of the Civil War, they'd developed two forms: closed (all cards dealt face-down) and open (some cards face-down, the rest face-up). Draw Poker, which came first, is a closed game. Draw introduced the notions of drawing cards from the stock to improve your hand and a second round of betting. Stud Poker is an open game. Stud introduced hole cards, upcards, and many more rounds of betting.

Poker was wildly attractive to the average person, but not to the stuffy editors of 19th-century *Hoyle* books. The game doesn't appear in *Hoyle* until the 1880s. As late as 1897, a commentator (a Whist devotee, most likely) noted "The best clubs do not admit the game to their rooms."

Though the Poker family is the second-most populous in all of card-dom (dwarfed only by Solitaire), all Poker variants have these traits in common:

1. Players try to build combinations based on the same rank, the same suit, or a numerical sequence.
2. All variations use a 52-card deck (not counting Jokers).
3. All suits are of equal value.
4. The cards rank from the Ace down to the 2. The Ace can be considered low to form a straight, and a straight can "turn a corner" (for example, K-A-1-2-3).
5. Each deal is a game-within-a-game.
6. Each deal features a pot, consisting of the total of the ante (the "entry fee") and all subsequent bets.
7. There's at least one round of betting.
8. The "best" hand wins the pot (the best can sometimes be the worst).
9. The object of Poker has never changed. In the words of David Parlett, it's to "bluff your opponents into thinking you hold the best combination whether you do or not, and then charge them for seeing it."

How the game is played

Any number from two to eight can play. The object of the game is to put together a better "poker hand" than the other players. These are the rankings of poker hands, from highest to lowest:

Five of a Kind	Only possible with a wild card
Straight Flush	Five cards in suit and in sequence
Four of a Kind	Four cards of any rank; one extra card
Full House	Three of a Kind plus One Pair
Flush	Five cards of the same suit
Straight	Five cards in sequence
Three of a Kind	Three cards of the same rank; two extra cards
Two Pairs	One Pair and One Pair; one extra card
One Pair	Two cards of the same rank; three extra cards
No Pair or "High-Card"	Any hand not meeting the above specs

The players bet to see who has the best hand. Each deal is a separate game, as its result doesn't affect any other deal. All the bets are placed together, forming the "pot." The object is to win the pot, whether by actually holding the best hand or by inducing other players to "fold" (drop out) and leave the pot to be taken, uncontested, by a single player still willing to bet.

The opportunity to bet passes clockwise from player to player. Once a player folds, the turn skips him or her and continues with the next player still in the action.

After betting is completed, each player can discard up to three cards, which the dealer immediately replaces. A second round of betting ensues, followed by a showdown; each player who has not previously folded shows what's in his or her hand. The highest-ranking hand at that point wins the pot.

In each betting interval, you can do one of four things:

Fold: Leave the hand

Call: Place in the pot only enough chips to stay in play for that betting interval

Raise: Place in the pot enough chips to call, plus additional chips

Check: A "bet of nothing," only possible when no previous player has made a bet in that betting interval. Checking allows a player to stay in the pot without risking additional chips.

When two players have hands of the same type, the higher-ranking hand is determined as follows:

—If each player has a Straight Flush, a Flush, a Straight, or No Pair, the hand with the highest card wins.

—If each has Five of a Kind, a Full House, Four of a Kind, or Three of a Kind, the hand composed of the highest-ranking matches wins.

—If each player has Two Pair, the highest pair wins. If each has the same higher pair, the hand with the higher of the two lower pairs wins. If each has the same two pairs, the hand with the higher fifth card wins.

—If the players have exactly identical hands, they split the pot.

Strategies

The power of a particular Poker hand (e.g., three 5s) is determined in part by the number of opponents you face. On average, if you're one of four Poker players, you'll win one of four hands, and three 5s is a great hand. If you're one of seven players, you'll only win one of seven hands, and three 5s is only a good hand.

In the default game, you're playing as one of eight. To win against such a large group, you'll need a pretty good hand to put the kibosh on all of them. More than likely, at least one of the others will have a high Pair, Two Pair, or Three of a Kind. This fact makes it very hard to win by bluffing.

Take a look at **Fig. 1**. Your hand, an "Ace high," is pretty weak. In a seven-player game, you're not going to win unless you draw a Pair (an Ace or other card). You can always scare some people out by betting high, but chances are you'll just be losing money. Try to hold down the bet by checking.

CHECK

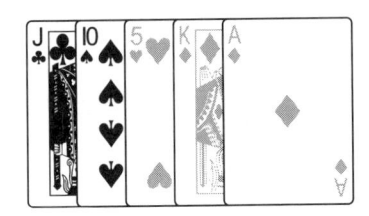

Fig 1: Seven-player game

However, if you do decide to bluff, try to do it when you're one of the last to bet. Otherwise, your bluff may be wasted against an opponent with a good hand who takes your bet and raises it.

Fig. 2 shows a different situation, in which a little bluffing is warranted. You may not win with your two Kings, but it might be helpful to drive some competitors out. You can often do this by betting a little more.

Fig. 2: Betting

Keep tabs on which player or players are doing the most betting. It will help you evaluate their hands when it's time to draw new cards.

DRAW 1   DRAW 3
FOLD   DRAW 2
FOLD   DRAW 3

Fig. 3: Drawing cards

Fig. 3 shows what happens next in this hypothetical hand. Your best choice is clear—keep the two Kings, and draw three more cards. The observant Poker player will watch the others with a keen eye. Two players fold and go out, as shown. One player draws one card. When a player draws one card, they most likely have Two Pair (a strong hand), or they might be going for a Straight or a Flush. The only tip-off for you that might indicate a Two Pair is whether they were betting heavily. With a strong hand, they probably raised the pot at least once. With a near-Straight or a near-Flush, they might have tried to keep the bets down by checking or calling.

Two other players (like yourself) draw three cards. The best possible hand you can have when drawing three cards is One Pair. Keep that in mind.

One player draws two cards, a more difficult play to interpret. This player has Three of a Kind or is bluffing. You draw three cards, the result of which is shown in **Fig. 4**. You fail to draw a third King. With fewer players, this might win you the hand. But with four opponents hanging in there, it would be unlikely. The best thing to do is to stay in with a minimal bet or fold.

Fig. 4: Bluffing

Hoyle® Card Games

If you are dealt a good opening hand (**Fig. 5**), your strategy should change. In this case, with three 10s, consider a lower bet, perhaps raising it once. This is like "dangling a worm" in front of your opponents and trying to make them bite. If you bet too high, it's the equivalent of splashing in the water; you'll scare away the fish. After the second round of betting starts, you can afford to bet a little higher.

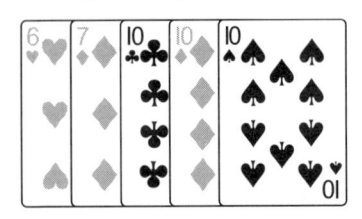

Fig. 5: Betting with a good hand

If you start winning some hands and getting ahead, you have the option of betting higher. While risky, this is likely to drive a couple people out; they just can't afford to hang in unless they have a great hand. Fewer opponents, of course, will improve your odds of winning.

SOLITAIRE

How the game evolved

Solitaire games exist in hundreds, if not thousands, of variations. All follow one of two principles: you're either building sequences by adding cards on top of foundation cards, or you're subtracting cards from the opening tableau. Subtraction games form the majority of Solitaires and were the most popular in the 1800s. Today, the addition games rule.

Whether adding or subtracting, winning (making the game "come out") depends on two things—choice and information. In most subtraction games, your choices are limited (if you have any at all beyond "playing it as it lays"). In most addition games, you have much more leeway in what you can and can't do. In those games, the more cards you can read, the more analytical the game becomes.

It may be possible to become too analytical. In *The Games Treasury*, Merilyn Simonds Mohr recounts the saga of Lewis Sutter of New York, a retiree who happily buckled down to the task of playing Solitaire on the first day he woke up and didn't have to go to work. Ten years later, Sutter had played 150,000 hands and had recorded every game in 10 accounting ledgers. To each his own...

Hoyle® Card Games

Tarot Lite

Solitaire first appeared in print as "Cabale" in a German games book in 1783. According to Mohr, "Patience" (the English name for Solitaire games) was first designed as a lighthearted way to foretell the future. In the late 18th century, the people of Denmark, Norway, and Iceland were also playing Cabale, a word that approximately means "secret knowledge." We know the first reliable report of fortune-telling with Tarot cards appeared in 1765, so it seems likely that Solitaire (Cabale) was originally intended to be a sort of "Tarot Lite."

The first book entirely devoted to Patience was published in Moscow in 1826. Six more books appeared before 1850, all of them in one of the Scandinavian languages or in Polish. This seems to point toward an origin somewhere in or near the Baltics. The Swedes have been suggested more than once as the originators, but the evidence is not conclusive. Tolstoy's *War and Peace* (published in installments in the 1860s) has several references to Patience, one in a scene set in 1808. Tolstoy was a stickler for historic detail and most likely would not have used the game in this way if he hadn't had a source to back it up.

The English learn Patience

We can assume that Cabale was unknown in England before the 1800s, as it never appeared in the Gamester books of the 1600s and 1700s. When the English did learn of Cabale, they christened it Patience, possibly because patience is the virtue these games were supposed to teach. (Anyone who's ever played the Klondike variation and been tempted to take just one peek knows these games also teach honor.)

The first English-language book on the subject came from an American, Annie B. Henshaw, in 1870: *Amusements for Invalids*. The title gives you an idea of the lack of respect Solitaire sometimes provokes. "Games for one player are childish and simple, and not worth learning," wrote one critic in *The Card Players Manual* of 1876. "When a man is reduced to such a pass as playing cards by himself, he had better give up!"

In England, Patience enjoyed a higher stature. Queen Victoria's husband, Prince Albert, was the most famous Patience devotee of the time (Albert was originally from Germany, where he'd played several versions of Cabale as a boy). In 1874, *The Illustrated Games of Patience* by Lady Adelaide Cadogan appeared, and the popularity of Patience soared. People began inventing new variants, which by the 1890s filled a seven-book series. The 1890s was the decade of the first travel agents and the first guided tours, and the compiler of those seven books, Mary Whitmore-Jones, was also the inventor of a special lap board for playing Patience while traveling.

The Great White North

When most Americans say they play Solitaire, they are referring to the popular Klondike variation. Klondike began as Canfield in Saratoga, New York. A saloon keeper there invented the game as a gambling mechanism to suck more money from his customers. (He later claimed that his roulette wheels were much more lucrative.) The customer paid $50 for a pack of cards and received $5 for each card he or she built on an Ace. Since five or six cards on the foundations is the average, the customer lost $20 to $25 per game. This sounds like a poor deal for the customer, and yet people flocked to play, trying for that big payoff.

When the Gold Rush to the Yukon Territory started in 1896, Canfield went along. It soon became associated with the entire phenomenon and was eventually dubbed Klondike, after that section of the Yukon Territory where gold was first discovered. "Described in one memoir as a 'vicious gambling Patience,' Klondike was undoubtedly responsible for a few fortunes changing hands," Mohr wrote.

So to summarize: Most Americans call Klondike Solitaire. In Britain this Patience is called Canfield. And back in America, the Solitaire we call Canfield is the Patience the British call Demon. (Got that?)

How the game is played

There are fifty different Solitaire games in Hoyle Card Games, including one-deck games, two-deck games, and arcade solitaire games (fast-paced games involving a time limit). All games are played by one player, except for Bowling, which can be played by up to four players. Rules for the Solitaire games are found in the online help.

Most Solitaire games involve playing cards from the tableau (card layout) to one or more foundations. Foundations are often (but not always) built up from Ace to King, in suit. Sometimes cards can be moved around the tableau; cards are usually moved in sequences, often by suit.

Strategies

Strategies for the Solitaire games are described below. Note that many games have game options you can change to make the games easier or harder; within a game, click Solitaire Settings on the Options menu to see what options are available.

One Deck Games

Aces Up: It is always good to play cards to the Foundation. Move Aces to empty columns when possible.

Baker's Dozen, Bristol: Move out your Aces to the Foundations as soon as possible, and get your lower cards out from under higher cards. Play cards of the same suit on your columns to make it easier to move them to Foundations as the game develops. In Baker's Dozen, uncovering cards is desirable.

Baroness: When there is more than one card combination you can remove (or two identical cards you can remove in combination with another card or cards), check to see if either will reveal cards you need to remove other cards; if so, remove that combination first.

Beleaguered Castle: Many of the tips for playing Klondike (see below) apply for this game as well. Try to empty out columns, so you can move Kings that cover needed cards.

Bowling: When first placing cards, be sure you leave gaps between them unless they're consecutive. (e.g., leave a gap between a 4 and a 6).

Betsy Ross, Calculation: Figure out what cards you'll need to play to the foundations early. Avoid covering up these cards. Don't lay a card over any lower card of the same rank. Consider reserving a column just for Kings.

Canfield, Eagle Wing: Play cards from the reserve before playing cards from the Waste pile whenever possible. Get your cards to the Foundations at every opportunity.

Clock: There are no choices to make in Clock, so you'll just have to hope that the cards are laid out to come out correctly. Making Clock come out is a very rare occurrence.

Cribbage Square: When placing the cards, remember what card combinations go best with others. Keep 7s and 8s in rows or columns, 5s with 10s and face cards. Try to score on double runs (e.g., 4, 5, 6, 6) and on 15s.

Eight Off, Flower Garden, Four Free, Seahaven Towers: Work to get the Aces and low cards out of the columns and over to the Foundations. When you find a move, perform it mentally to see where you end up. Then compare it to your other possible moves to see which one does the most good. This is important, because you can end up limiting your options if you're not careful. Try to empty columns to increase your mobility.

Eliminator: Every empty Foundation can be used to avoid a dead-end. Therefore, try to use as few Foundations as possible. Look for runs of cards in suit, especially for the longest run in the first moves of the game. **Fig. 1** shows an example of this. By playing the 3 and the 10 to the Foundations, you unlock six other cards (the 4, 5, 6, 7, J, Q). Conversely, the 4 and the 7 only unlock one card (the 3).

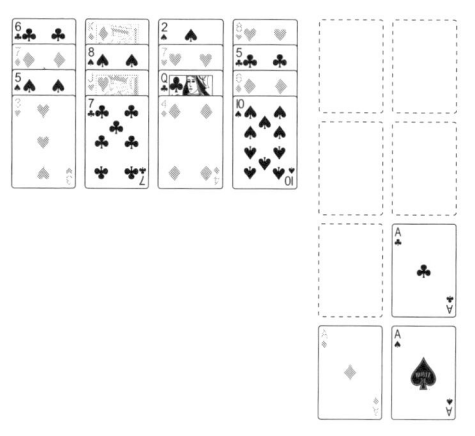

Fig. 1: Unlocking cards

Euchre: You want to be able to choose a trump suit so that there will be a good chance your hand will win at least three tricks. If you choose the trump suit of the upcard, keep in mind that this card will be the first card played by the deck.

High trump cards and Aces of other suits should have good chances to win tricks. Low trump cards may also win tricks if you are void in other suits. During play, if you don't have a sure winner but have low trump cards, throw away weak singleton non-trumps so you can later trump that suit.

Fortress, Shamrocks: To decide on the starting card for the Foundations, look at the top half of the columns to see which cards are most prevalent. If there are a lot of cards of similar rankings (e.g., 5s, 6s, and 7s), pick the lower rank (5s in this example) for the Foundations, since you're building up. Build up the Foundations evenly.

Since any card can be placed in an empty column, you will increase your options if you can pile lots of cards in relatively few columns. In Shamrocks, stay away from building columns upwards (e.g., 3, 4, 5 with 5 on top), as you won't be able to move the lower card to the Foundation.

Four Seasons: Since you can fill empty spaces at any time, wait to fill a space with a card you'll need soon, rather than filling it right away. Note that you can lift any card from a Tableau pile to "peek" under it and see what card (if any) is underneath.

Gaps: You'll have big trouble if you leave a gap to the right of a King. Ditto if you allow a gap to shift to the far right end of a row.

Golf: Before playing, check to see which card sequences will permit the highest number of cards to be moved to the Foundation. Save your 2s and Queens as insurance against an Ace or King that turns up from the stock.

Klondike: Before your first play, flip the card from the stock to see what's available. However, don't play any cards from here except as a last resort. Make it your intention to uncover the cards hidden beneath the columns (if you can get these out, you will usually win). Whatever play creates the most card movement between columns (thus, building sequences) and results in flipping a hidden card will be the best move you can make.

Before making a move, mentally forecast where it will end up. If it ends up at a dead end, look for something else. In **Fig. 2**, for example, you can move either 10 onto the Jack, but to uncover a card and avoid a dead end, you need to move the 10 of Clubs. Build your Foundations up evenly when possible.

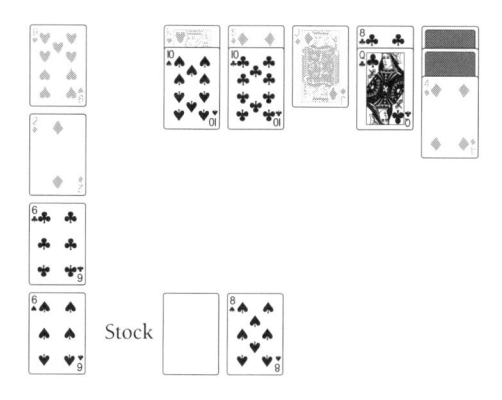

Fig. 2: Avoiding dead ends

La Belle Lucie: Check to see what top cards in the columns can be moved to the Foundations first. Once you've exhausted these options, try to free up other cards that can be moved to the Foundation. Any sequence of two cards of the same suit on a column are stuck (i.e., the higher card on the bottom can't be moved), so you should avoid building sequences in columns except when it frees up a card for the Foundation. Once you are forced to build a sequence on a column, go ahead and stack up any additional cards that are available.

Nestor: Match pairs from the Tableau before taking cards from the Reserve. Take cards that will unlock additional pairs. Never match a pair from the Reserve; this doesn't help you at all. Just wait until they can be matched with a cards from the Tableau.

Penguin: Strategy for Penguin is similar to Four Free. Uncover low cards as soon as possible, and move them to the Foundations.

Poker Square: Try to build Straights and Flushes in one direction (vertically or horizontally) and build Pairs, Three of a Kind, Four of a Kind, etc. in the opposite direction. Pairs and Two Pairs are worth so few points that, toward the end of the game you should avoid forming these combinations, unless you have no choice.

Pyramid, Scorpion: First, try to match cards from the tableau. Then match them with cards from the Stock if possible. In Pyramid, save the cards in the Reserve as a last resort when you no longer have any plays.

Slide: Before sliding any cards, look carefully at your grid to see if there are any easy matches (three slides or less) Be sure you're not wasting many moves on low-ranking cards, especially late in the game when you're scoring on bigger multipliers. You only have 12 moves, so make them count.

Spiderette, Yukon: As in Klondike, your best moves are those that uncover hidden cards, so play accordingly. Because there is no redeal in Spiderette, complete all possible moves in the Tableau before choosing cards from the Stock.

Strategy: It is critical to avoid placing a card on a stack that already contains another lower-ranking card of the same suit. Place lower cards on top of higher cards generally. Ideally, if you can get four consecutive cards of one rank together (e.g., four Jacks), that will help later. If you can get three or four consecutive cards of one rank together, begin placing cards of the next lowest rank right on top of these (note the Kings in **Fig. 3**). This game is easier to manage if you place lower cards on one side and move up to the higher cards on the other side. In Fig. 3, you should play the Queen of Diamonds on the King. Otherwise, you will be blocking the 10 or the Jack of Diamonds. By saving an end row for Kings, you avoid trouble later.

Fig. 3: Placing cards

Triplets: In order to win, your first set must determine all your subsequent sets (e.g., if you select a 3, 4, 5, try to obtain a K, A, 2, a 6, 7, 8, and so on). Try to pull one card from each rank before taking a second card from any rank, and take all your second cards before third cards, etc. When you have options in your selections (e.g., two 9s are available), take the one that covers a card you'll need to match in the next few plays. Avoid taking the bottom card in a pile unless there are no other cards of the same rank available elsewhere.

Two Deck Games

Aces and Kings: Moving a card from an Ace Foundation to a King Foundation (or vice versa) makes it possible to play different cards to the Foundations. For instance, moving a Jack from the top of a Queen (on the King Foundation) to the top of a 10 (on the Ace Foundation) makes it possible to play a Queen to the Foundations, instead of a 10.

If you can choose between moving a card with the same rank from the Reserve piles or the Tableau piles, it is usually better to move it from the Reserve piles, since that frees up other cards you might need.

Alhambra: Be sure not to miss any possible plays to the Waste pile, since this is the only way to move cards between piles.

If you have a choice to play two identical cards on the Reserve piles, "peek" under the piles to see which cards are underneath to decide which card to play.

Batsford: This game is the same as Klondike except for the number of cards and columns used and the ability to place three Kings in a Reserve pile. The Reserve pile is most useful to get Kings out of the Stock pile, since there is no redeal; it's usually best not to move Kings from the Tableau to the Reserve pile unless really needed.

Be sure to get Kings out of the Reserve pile out at the earliest opportunity, since the pile can only hold three Kings, and there are eight in the pile.

Colorado: Remember that you can lift any card from a Tableau pile to "peek" under it and see what card (if any) is underneath. In general, try to place cards on tops of piles of cards of the same suit. Then, when you remove a card from a pile, you might be able to use the card under it in the future. But try not to cover up cards that you'll need soon.

If two of the Tableau piles hold the same card (rank and suit), you might want to cover one of those piles with a card, since you are unlikely to need both cards at the same time.

Forty Thieves: This is a very difficult game to finish, since you can only build the Tableau columns down in suit. As much as possible, try to free up the Aces. When given a choice of two identical cards to play to a Foundation, play a card that will let you free up better cards underneath.

Mount Olympus: It may take some time to get used to building down the Tableau by twos in suit; make sure you don't miss any plays before you flip over a new card (to quickly check these, right-click (Ctrl+click on the Macintosh) each card to automatically move it). As with Forty Thieves, when given a choice of two identical cards to play to a Foundation, play a card that will let you free up better cards underneath.

Red and Black: This game is interesting in that building to the Tableau sets you up for building to the Foundations, so careful building is imperative. Remember when moving cards on the Tableau that you can only move one card at a time, so if there are multiple cards in a sequence, you should move the highest cards first. (In other words, if you have a red nine, a black eight, and a red seven on three different columns, move the black eight onto the red nine first, then move the red seven onto the eight; if you move the red seven onto the black eight first, you won't be able to move the seven and eight onto the nine.)

Whenever possible, play all of the cards in a column, since empty columns get filled by the upcard of the Stock pile; this gives you more cards to play with on the Tableau.

Spider: Use the same strategies as Spiderette; see the "One Deck Games" section.

Sultan: Since you can fill the empty Tableau piles at any time, you might want to wait to fill a pile with a card you'll need soon, rather than filling it right away.

Terrace: Critical to the success of this game is picking a good initial card to start the Foundations. Look at the Reserve pile to see which cards will be available soon, and which won't. For instance, if there are two 5s buried deep in the Reserve pile, 5 (or 4, or 3) may not be a good choice as a starting rank for the Foundations.

Arcade Games

3 Towers: If possible, choose cards in the Tableau that form long sequences, because you get more points that way. Otherwise, choose cards that maximize the number of other cards in the tableau that will become exposed.

Best 21: Try to form piles of 11, since cards with the value 10 are the most common. Of course, you'll want to use your Aces on piles of 10 or 20.

Fast 21: Use the same strategies as for Best 21. Also, if you don't have a good place to put low cards, keep them in a separate hand to try to form 5-card Charlies.

Pick 2: When possible, remove pairs instead of sequences, since you get more points for pairs. Choose pairs and sequences in such a way that favorable cards will become exposed.

Sum 11: Be on the lookout for all the different ways cards can add up to 11: 5-6, 7-4, 8-3, 9-2, 10-A, 6-3-A-A, and so on. Remove cards in such a way that as many other cards as possible are exposed.

SPADES

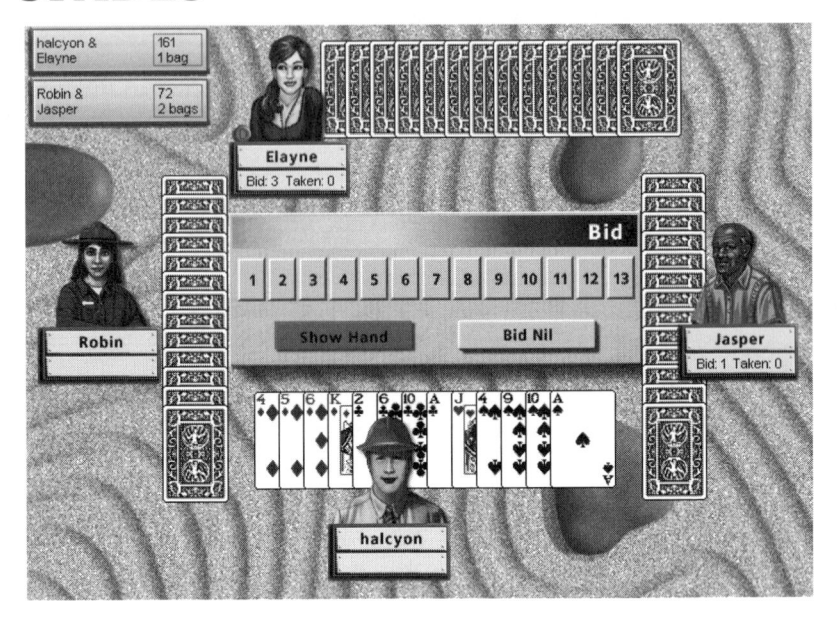

How the game evolved

Spades was most likely developed simultaneously with Whist as a simpler form of that game. Whereas Whist was replaced by Bridge, nothing ever came along to replace Spades. According to the USPCC, (United States Playing Card Co.) Spades ranks as the number-one card game among American college students.

How the game is played

Spades is played by four people in two partnerships. The cards rank Ace (the highest) to the 2 (the lowest). Spades are always trumps.

Each player receives 13 cards. Bidding and play proceed in a clockwise direction. In the bidding phase you declare the number of tricks you intend to win; in the playing phase you try to win those tricks. The object of the game is to fulfill the total bid by the partnership.

You may choose to bid "Nil," meaning you intend not to win any tricks. Before you even pick up your cards, you may bid Double Nil. This is the same as a Nil bid, except all rewards and penalties are doubled. If one or both players in a partnership bid Nil, their bids are scored independently, then combined to determine the partnership's score.

You must follow suit if you can, otherwise you may take the trick with a trump or discard something from a non-trump suit. Spades cannot be lead until they've been "broken" (until they've been used to trump an earlier lead). A trick is won by the highest trump or by the highest card of the suit led.

If you make your bid, you receive 10 points for each trick in the bid, one point for each trick above the bid. A Nil bid counts for 100 points if you succeed, 100 against if you fail. Double Nil is 200. The game is to 500 points.

Not all Spades games use "bags," but ours does. Every point in excess of your total bid counts as one bag. If you collect 10 bags, you lose 100 points.

Strategies

Try to estimate the number of tricks you'll take as accurately as possible. Count Kings and Aces as one trick each. The value of your lower-ranking trumps depends on the presence of voids, singletons, or doubletons in your off-suits (non-trumps). For example, if you have three low trumps (**Fig. 1**) and one doubleton (two Clubs), you can expect your trumps to take one trick.

Fig. 1: Value of trumps

If you have a similar hand, but a singleton (one Club) instead, you can expect to take two tricks with your low trumps. With three trumps and a void in one suit, you might take three tricks. Additional trump cards above three are worth one trick each on average.

If someone else is bidding Nil, that will make it easier for you to win tricks, and you might consider adding one trick to your estimation. In a perfect world, the total amount of tricks bid in each hand of Spades should equal 13, since there are 13 tricks to be won.

If you are the third or last player to bid, consider how the other players have been bidding. If the bid count is low, you may want to include marginal cards (such as a pair of Queens) as one trick.

Bid Nil, obviously, if you're pretty sure you won't be taking any tricks. Some danger signs to look for in your hand are a suit of three or fewer cards that contains any high-cards. In the example shown in **Fig. 2**, the King of Diamonds is the primary threat to a successful Nil bid. Even if the King is saved for the third Diamond trick, no one else (except your partner) will trump it, and you'll take the trick.

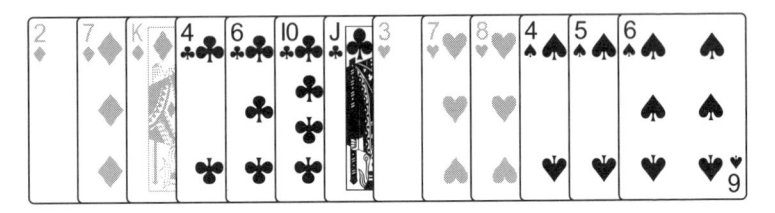

Fig. 2: When to bid Nil

The exception to this is when you have a void or a singleton in a suit. In this case, there's a good chance you can dump the King harmlessly before you take a trick.

If you have a hand that's long in Spades (four or more), it is very unlikely you can carry out a successful Nil bid (those Spades will be the implements used to dig your grave). You're bound to win a trick, costing you 100 points.

Your strategy during play should depend somewhat on the total bid for tricks that will be taken. If the total bid is very high (12 or more tricks), you need to be aggressive. Fight for tricks, throw off low cards whenever possible. Avoid taking any tricks from your partner. By doing so, you may prevent your opponents from fulfilling their contract. Also, with a high total bid, it is unlikely you'll be taking many bags for your team, no matter what.

Spades is like Hearts in one respect: sometimes it's better to lose tricks. If the bid is low (10 or less), you should avoid taking any tricks you hadn't counted on. For example, with the cards shown in **Fig. 3**, you can take the trick by playing your Jack of Clubs. If the total bid is only 10, you should play your 8 to lose the trick. This will help you to avoid acquiring bags from overbidding. You also needn't worry as much about taking your partner's tricks.

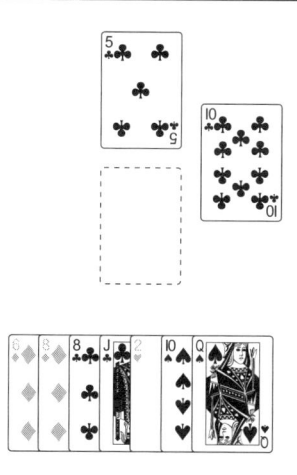

Fig. 3: Avoiding tricks on a low bid

What if the total bid for tricks is exactly 11? In this case, base your play on other factors. If you have accumulated only a few bags, try to win the tricks at first. Change this strategy as circumstances dictate. You can increase your options in later tricks by playing your middle cards early. Take a look at **Fig. 4**. If you bid three tricks yourself, and you just need two more tricks to fulfill your contract, consider playing the 7 of Diamonds. This will give you flexibility later. The next time Diamonds are led, you can evaluate whether you need to lose a trick by playing your 2 or to win it with your Queen.

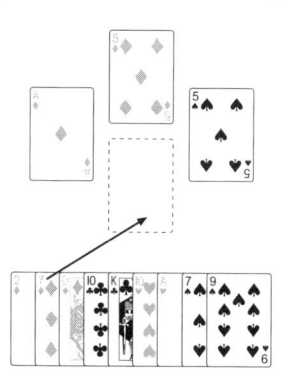

Fig. 4: Playing middle cards

Another tactic you can use when trying to make your bid is to watch your partner's plays closely. If he or she inadvertently loses a trick that's normally a win (for example, if your partner gets trumped early), try to make it up by taking one trick above your own bid.

Hoyle® Card Games

If an opponent bids Nil, you will need to make sure that he or she takes one trick. To do this, play the lowest cards possible, and don't worry about fulfilling your contract (assuming the total bid is low, which is probable). Save your low cards specifically for trying to stick the Nil bidder. This is exemplified in **Fig. 5**. The Nil bidder is on the right. Your partner will win the trick. You should save the 3 of Clubs, and play the 9 of Clubs.

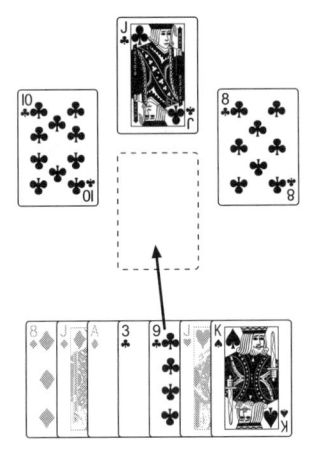

Fig. 5: Stopping Nil

WAR

How the game evolved

War is a game with no recorded history. Card scholars of the past three centuries are silent on this subject. Even the *Hoyle* books confine themselves to a recitation of the rules rather than an illumination of how War came to be.

Most children's card games are offshoots from adult games, and War seems to be no exception. The game is aptly named, as its mechanism of play replicates the single-warrior combat of an earlier time—instead of my knight versus your knight, in War, it's my card versus your card, and only one card can win.

That's the adult element. The kid element is in the time required to play War. It takes a *long* time to win all 52 cards from your opponent—just what a weary parent needs when two children must be kept entertained.

How the game is played

War is played between two players. They split a standard 52-card pack. Each of the combatants turns up a card. The player whose card is higher (suits don't matter) wins both cards and places them at the bottom of his or her pack.

Play continues until a pair is turned up, at which point you declare "War." The two cards of the pair are placed in the center, and each player plays three cards face-down ("W-A-R") and a fourth face-up ("spells War!"). The player who plays the higher face-up card wins all the cards in the war, unless the two cards again form a pair—in that case, you must have another war. (A player with insufficient cards remaining to fill out this procedure puts down as many cards as he or she has left. The opposition matches this number.) The object of the game is to win all the cards.

FURTHER READING ON CARD GAMES

Vernon Bartlett, *The Past of Pastimes* (1969)

Henry G. Francis, Alan F. Truscott, and Dorothy A. Francis (eds.), *The Official Encyclopedia of Bridge* (5th edition, 1994)

Frederic Grunfeld (editor), *Games of the World* (1975)

Catherine Perry Hargrave, *A History of Playing Cards* and *A Bibliography of Cards and Gaming* (1930)

Oswald Jacoby & Albert Morehead (editors), *The Fireside Book of Cards* (1957)

> *The Fireside Book of Cards* includes the essays "The Origin of Gaming and Cards" and "The Reign of Hoyle" by Catherine Perry Hargrave, "Designs of the Face Cards" by Robert Hutchings, "Who Is Hoyle?" by Richard L. Frey, excerpts from *The Complete Book of Solitaire and Patience Games* by Albert Morehead and Geoffrey Mott-Smith, and "The Origin of Contract Bridge" by Harold S. Vanderbilt.

Merilyn Simonds Mohr, *The New Games Treasury* (1993)

Albert Morehead & Geoffrey Mott-Smith (editors), *Hoyle's Rules of Games* (1983)

Albert Morehead, Richard L. Frey, & Geoffrey Mott-Smith, *The New Complete Hoyle Revised* (1991)

H.T. Morley, *Old and Curious Playing Cards: Their History and Types from Many Countries and Periods* (1931)

Jack Olsen, *The Mad World of Bridge* (1960)

David Parlett, *The Penguin Book of Card Games* (1979), *A History of Card Games* (1990), *A Dictionary of Card Games* (1992), and *Teach Yourself Card Games for One* (1994)

And on the Web, **www.pagat.com** is an extensive card games site, with information about card games from all over the world.

SIERRA ON-LINE TECHNICAL SUPPORT

North America
    Sierra On-Line, Inc.
    Technical Support
    P.O. Box 85006
    Bellevue, WA 98015-8506

    Main: (425) 644-4343
    Monday-Friday, 8:00 a.m.- 4:45 p.m. PST
    Fax: (425) 644-7697

    http://www.sierra.com
    support@sierra.com

United Kingdom
    Havas Interactive
    2 Beacontree Plaza,
    Gillette Way,
    Reading, Berkshire
    RG2 0BS United Kingdom

    Main: (0118) 920-9111
    Monday-Friday, 9:00 a.m. - 5:00 p.m.
    Fax: (0118) 987-5603

    http://www.sierra-online.co.uk

France
    Havas Interactive France
    32, Av de l'Europe
    Bât Energy 1 (2e étage)
    78 140 VELIZY-Villacoublay
    France

    Téléphone: 01-30-67-90-50
    Lundi au Jeudi de 10h à 19h
    Vendredi de 10h à 18h
    Fax: 01 30 67 90 65

    http://www.sierra.fr

Germany
> Havas Interactive
> Robert-Bosch-Str. 32
> D-63303 Dreieich
> Deutschland
>
> Tel: (0) 6103-99-40-40
> Montag bis Freitag von 9 - 19Uhr
> Fax/Mailbox: (0) 6103-99-40-35
>
> http://www.sierra.de

Spain
> Havas Interactive
> Avenida de Burgos 9
> 1°-OF2
> 28036 Madrid
> Spain
>
> Teléfono: (01) 383-2623
> de lunes a Viernes de 09:30 a 15:00 y de 16:00 a 18:30
> Fax: 91 381 24 37

Italy

Contattare il vostro distribotore.

NOTES